Negotiating
New
York

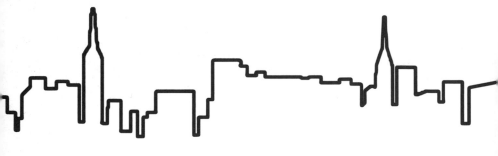

Negotiating New York

Life, Love, and the Pursuit of Real Estate

Joanne R. Douglas
with Alfred Renna

BEYOND WORDS

Hillsboro, Oregon

BEYOND WORDS

20827 N.W. Cornell Road, Suite 500
Hillsboro, Oregon 97124-9808
503-531-8700 / 503-531-8773 fax
www.beyondword.com

First Beyond Words paperback edition September 2017
Copyright © 2017 by Joanne R. Douglas and Alfred Renna

Beyond Words Publishing is an imprint of Simon & Schuster, Inc., and the Beyond Words logo is a registered trademark of Beyond Words Publishing, Inc.

For information about special discounts for bulk purchases, please contact Beyond Words Special Sales at 503-531-8700 or specialsales@beyondword.com.

Managing Editor: Lindsay S. Easterbrooks-Brown
Editor: Nevin Mays
Copyeditors: Gretchen Stelter, Henry Covey
Proofreader: Michelle Blair
Design: Devon Smith
Composition: William H. Brunson Typography Services
The text of this book was set in Minion Pro.

Manufactured in the United States of America

10 9 8 7 6 5 4 3 2 1

Library of Congress Cataloging-in-Publication Data
Names: Douglas, Joanne R., author. | Renna, Alfred, author.
Title: Negotiating New York : life, love, and the pursuit of real estate /
  Joanne R. Douglas with Alfred Renna.
Description: Hillsboro, Oregon : Beyond Words Pub., [2017]
Identifiers: LCCN 2017007275 | ISBN 9781582706344 (pbk.) |
ISBN 97815827066894 (eBook)
Subjects: LCSH: Real estate agents—New York (State) | House selling—New York (State) |
  Real estate business—New York (State)
Classification: LCC HD278 .D68 2017 | DDC 333.3092/27471—dc23
LC record available at https://lccn.loc.gov/2017007275

The corporate mission of Beyond Words Publishing, Inc.: *Inspire to Integrity*

Dedicated to our parents, Millie and Al.
Still in love and dancing in heaven.

Contents

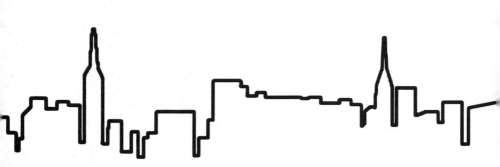

Foreword

First let me say this, Alfred Renna makes me laugh. I first got to know Alfred well when I hired him as a sales manager. Then I sent him to Columbia University to learn about computer systems when I knew he would be the perfect person to help bring my growing real estate company into the twenty-first-century. I drove him crazy turning down photo after photo that he suggested for our very first website home page. It had to be perfect. It would become the first recognized real estate website in Manhattan and probably the whole country. "And don't use my photo," was my only instruction.

One day he came into my office with a poster-size board and asked that I have an open mind before turning it around. There I was, looking gorgeous, I might add. I couldn't help blurting out, "I love it, let's use it!" Alfred was ecstatic he could finally launch our site, as this was the last piece he needed. He walked out of my office laughing. "Hey," I called after him. "Come back here. What are you laughing at?"

"Don't be mad at me," he said as he turned around, his face turning red. "I had the photo manipulated a little, these aren't your legs." No wonder I looked like a model.

A few years later, Alfred's sister and brother-in-law, Joanne Douglas and her husband Jonathan Douglas joined the company. I was always happy to see them when passing by their desks on my way to the office, especially Jonathan because he was so handsome and he reminded me of my first boyfriend. I liked them as much as I had become so fond of Alfred. There is something about the Rennas that just makes you want to hang out around the kitchen table with the whole family.

When I sold my company, the hardest part was leaving so many wonderful people behind. So, when I heard that Joanne and Alfred had written a book, a fun book, about life, love, and real estate, I couldn't wait to read it. *Negotiating New York* is really fun, and as they say in publishing it's "a great read". It is enjoyable and insightful from amazing real estate sagas to pitch perfect portrayals of wonderful New York centric characters. Reading about the Rennas, from their parents, Millie and Al, to their sisters, cousins, and friends, reminds me so much of my own life, also overflowing with wonderful family and friends.

From tears to laughter, I felt like I was right there with the Renna clan, racing about New York City, meeting crazy buyers and eccentric sellers, stopping at their favorite cafés and restaurants, and learning their tips on making lots of money, some of which I'm sure they learned from me! Most especially, I love the wonderful stories, and how much they stick together, like how they squabble, then take a breath, and head off to dinner together! I love it.

Negotiating New York is also about how healing laughter can be. You will see how the family grieved from the passing of Jonathan, after a tough battle, to the deaths of their parents, and how being able to laugh healed them.

This is a wonderful, life-affirming story about four siblings living and working in the big city, but they might as well be from a small Midwestern town, or as we say in Manhattan, from the other side of the river. We were all from the other side of the river, with the Manhattan skyline beckoning to us to come and work hard and make it big.

As the pride I feel with my *Shark Tank* entrepreneurs, I am proud of Alfred and Joanne. It is wonderful to see how those who have worked for me have grown; Alfred maturing into an amazing and popular manager, working with hundreds of agents, and Joanne growing The Douglas Team into one of the most successful in the city, and I am so proud of the success I see for them with *Negotiating New York: Life, Love, and the Pursuit of Real Estate.*

—Barbara Corcoran,
star of the 2015 and 2014 Emmy Award winning show, *Shark Tank*,
and author of *New York Times* bestseller *Shark Tales*

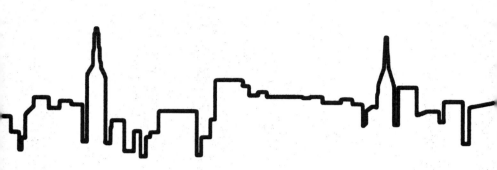

Introduction:
Open House!

Donna was wringing her hands about the offer she had made on the fabulous '50s beach bungalow. It was her first real estate purchase, and it was a house in the Hamptons. While it was not right on the beach, it was right by the beach. We all had to keep it a big secret. In real estate, you don't talk about what you're about to buy until the day you close, because word gets around and suddenly another buyer wants it and just might try to snatch it out from under you. Donna, not only the last born of our family, was also the last to own her own piece of the pie, and this first purchase was the luxury of a weekend house.

"I'm the only one who doesn't have my own house," she would often remind us, her voice going up an octave. Alfred had perfected her high-pitch complaint when he'd imitate her.

So the pending purchase was momentous. She was excited, we all were excited, and we all went to inspect the house before she agreed to the final offer.

"It was an apocalypse," Alfred recalled later. "We converged on that house like a SWAT team. It was the whole family."

My three siblings and I (Donna, Alfred, and Rosemary) are also known collectively as the Rennas, though we have been called various other names. One in particular has a certain ring to it: the Rennavators, which sounds like a singing group, which we're not. We don't even sing that well except for Donna, and the rest of us are best at making a joyful noise, as the old proverb says. What we so love, love, love is real estate: the architecture of houses old and new, big and small. But the best parts for us are the bidding, buying, selling . . . and then doing it all over again. Oh, that's on the weekends, 'cause we all have jobs. It just happens three of us—Alfred, Donna, and I—work full-time in the real estate business in Manhattan, and Rosemary sort of works part-time in real estate, sometimes showing properties for us, sometimes traveling to manage her own investment properties, and, the rest of the time, indulging in her favorite work-related activity: decorating and staging. For that, she will help any one of us with her fine talents. All combined—throw in a few apartments, a teensy partnership in what is referred to as a *fund* that specializes in buying and managing apartment buildings, pieces of land here and there, various rental properties, weekend houses, Rosemary's Italian palazzo in Ortigia, a small island off the coast of Sicily—all combined we have quite the diversified portfolio that we are always looking to expand. Most of our real estate investment endeavors have been quite profitable and fun, whether our own homes, properties for rental income, or those to flip for profit. Ortigia was the *Under the Tuscan Sun* renovation nightmare that was Rosemary's full-time job for three years. We all love the thrill and torment of it all. We've got one kid between the four of us,

Rosemary's son, Rico. He's got the bug too and has been calculating square footage since he was four. That about sums up why it seems like all we talk about is architecture, design, and real estate.

Our family circle morphed over recent years due to deaths, breakups, and new beginnings. We have cousins and various other ancillary family—lots of honorary brothers and sisters, and significant others and their families. Everyone loves to say they are one of us, "us" being the four siblings. Why? Who knows? We argue, we yell, we debate, we eat. Rosemary and Alfred were feuding for months over an apartment each had lived in at different times, debating which furnishings belonged to whom and who spent more money on renovating the kitchen. For the most part, the rest of us ignored them, but it was disconcerting at the time, because they hardly spoke to each other. But did they stop being in each other's company? No, they continued on in their obnoxious little feud. I think they were trying to out last one another. One weekend when I was at Alfred's house in Southampton, New York, I heard him call her on speakerphone, and they sure were curt, offering as few words as possible, and sounding as uninterested as possible, so as not to appear to be communicating with each other.

"Rosemary."

"What?"

"I'm making dinner."

"When?"

"Tonight. Seven."

"I'll be there."

"Oy," was all I could say—the shortened version of *oy vey ist mir*, the perfect Yiddish expression of exasperation. The day we went for the big preview of what would become Donna's weekend abode, I called Rosemary, who was in Ortigia, on FaceTime, and caught her in the middle of yelling in Italian to her third Sicilian contractor. (Thankfully, she and Alfred were back to more normal sibling spats.)

The three of us who were in the States arrived within moments of one another. That fortuitous day, counting Rosemary over the phone and the assistant, we were nine people, which meant there were five brokers as well as the four of us. We also had our real estate attorney, who happens to be our cousin Michael, another Renna. Then there was our in-house architect, whose name was also Michael, and who was Donna's boyfriend at the time. To differentiate, we referred to our cousin Michael as Cousin Michael, and Donna's Michael as Michael Amore because "amore" was Donna's pet name for him since she had been intensely studying Italian. Our builder is my amore who goes by Paul, but his first name is really James. Then there was our engineer, Paul's brother, Terry, who moved to the area shortly after Paul did.

Our cars were parked all over the narrow dirt road that had a sign at the entrance that said PRIVATE ROAD: NO TRESPASSING. The 850-square-foot casita with cottage detailing was sitting on a rise with towering pine trees. What it lacked in size, it made up in charm. I knew from the moment I stepped foot on the front lawn that Donna would buy this house. I even knew exactly at what price. It's a gift, you might say: real estate foreknowledge. That day, it manifested like a tingle that came up from the earth itself, prickling through me till it hit my brain. It was days before Donna felt it too and finally accepted the owner's lowest and best counteroffer. She had been a bit annoyed that my premonition had not been about $5,000 less.

"It feels like the Poconos," Alfred said immediately.

"Turn me around!" Rosemary's voice came out of my iPhone, asking me to turn the phone around so she could see. I had to agree; it looked like the Poconos, the well-known mountain resort area about two hours north of the city.

"But we are only two or three sips of wine from sand and water," I reminded everyone, and yet we were entranced and hadn't even made it to the front door. The listing broker's assistant looked like a deer in headlights as we all rustled past him and filed into the house.

Viewing Donna's potential house was such a great high; it was a perfect fixer-upper at a great price and had a tiny cottage out back that could eventually be a pool house. After scattering throughout the property to carefully inspect it, and all pronouncing and nodding our approvals—despite the rotting siding, creepy crawl space, and need for more guest space for our extended family—we all really wanted to keep up our house hunting high. The cottage was a tease and left us yearning for another real estate fix, but since house hunting is hard work, we were also getting hungry, so Paul and I jumped in the Jeep to head to Sag Harbor for sushi. Given the narrowness of the private road and all the cars, we had to drive to the end to turn around. That's when I saw the sign that always makes my heart beat faster.

"Open house!" I screeched. "Turn here. It's on the water!" Paul made the fast, sharp right, barely missing a big tree. I still had Rosemary on FaceTime.

"I want to see it too!" I heard as I disconnected her and pressed speed dial for Alfred's cell.

"Alfred, there's an open house right up the road!" Adrenaline pumping, I heard Alfred call out to everyone else.

"Get in the car!" followed by a moment of silence as I imagined they were all thinking, *Did something happen?* Then he shouted again, "OPEN HOUSE!"

In the next moment, there was a cloud of dust billowing up the road. Alfred's car swerved into the driveway and hadn't even come to a stop before the doors flew open and the members of our house touring group piled out. We converged again like a well-trained battalion marching across the wrap-around porch where we startled the listing broker.

"Hi, I'm Joanne R. Douglas. I'm a broker in the city."

By law, if you are a real estate broker in a real estate sort of scenario, you must identify yourself as such, with your full name as it appears on your license to sell. Then I attempted to introduce each member of our entourage as they stampeded through the house.

"The guy who just slammed the fuse box closed and is heading to the basement is our engineer, Terry..." but before I could get through the rest, the call to end the tour and head out sounded.

"This place is a teardown for sure." Cousin Michael announced, as he looked up at a gaping crack in the living room ceiling.

"Teardown!" Alfred yelled from the kitchen followed by the sounds of cabinet doors slamming closed. Like a shared signal, the conclusion moved on down the line.

"Terry Glenn, it's a teardown," Paul called down to his brother in the basement.

"Yup," we heard come back up. "It's a teardown all right."

Alfred, also the diplomat, said to the broker, "After viewing the house, we have concluded that it has a great bay view, and we love it, but it's a teardown." Now, we don't mind teardowns. Paul and I tore down to build our own house. We just weren't in the mood, and that week we craved something more like . . . *a fixer-upper.*

We were all gone just as fast as we had come, off to another neighborhood.

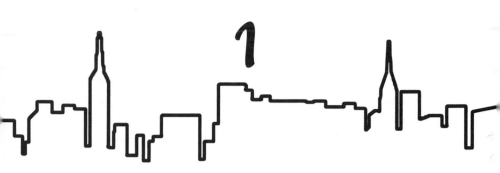

Beginnings

My husband, Jonathan Douglas, and I were the first married sales team in New York City by the time we joined the Corcoran Group in the fall of 2000, where we were aptly christened "The Douglas Team." Before that, we were with a smaller firm where we were finding our footing and attempting to grow. It was Jonathan who always had amazing foresight on the market and who, early on, suggested we hire our friend Lenny as an assistant. We were among the very first brokers in the business to make that addition to our two-person workforce. Certain we needed more good people to keep growing, Jonathan then insisted we hire someone to drive for us. I was concerned with our growing monthly expenses but gave in when he suggested we hire Ed, whom we had already met driving his own sedan for a car service that we used from time to time. Jonathan gave him a call, and Ed became a part of The Douglas Team, driving us and our customers all around town in our Blazer.

With the help of Lenny and Ed, our business took off. At Corcoran, we were able to increase that success with a wonderful marketing department that helped us create beautiful materials to promote our brand as well as the properties we represented. The thin, multicolor stripe band that was created for our team's marketing materials was later adopted by the new Corcoran Group as a part of their branding, so we moved on to something fresh and new for us.

As real estate agents and brokers, even though you are under the umbrella of a large company, you are an independent contractor; you might say you are a small company within a larger company. You get a commission from the sales you make, which is divided with the company you are affiliated with.

We loved the Corcoran Group back when Barbara Corcoran still owned it. Our desks were near her office, and she always made us feel very special. It's a gift she has with people. Soon after joining the Corcoran Group, we were invited to speak and teach with her at real estate seminars. She and Jonathan had a special bond, in part because they were both from large families. Also, Barbara said he looked like her first boyfriend! But Jonathan could read people and had a knack for predicting market trends, and Barbara recognized these traits in him and trusted his intuition when he shared industry insights with her. That intuition enabled me, the front person of our team, to negotiate with strength.

As we entered our sixth year with Corcoran, we were provided with more desks as our team grew, and they were now paying Lenny's salary. Our friend and team member Barbara Levey had joined from our last company. Jonathan knew my sister Donna would also be a perfect fit, as she was accustomed to precise work, speed, and extreme customer service. She had started her Wall Street career on a trading desk and loved the rapid pace. From there, she had joined a nationally known brokerage firm, where she spent eleven years building her portfolio of high-net-worth clientele. She was the highest producer in the New York office. However, aside from SEC rules, the rules of that firm infuriated her. One very frustrating rule was that everyone in the office received the same commissions and bonuses, regardless of if they brought in one dollar of investment or $50 million. Donna's income did not increase with her ever-expanding pool of investors, most of whom trusted her implicitly. She was ready to change careers, and we were hoping she would bring her contact list.

Donna's arrival meant there were three of us four Renna siblings under the same corporate roof, since Alfred was Corcoran's senior managing director then. Our team grew, as did our success. Jonathan and I had nothing when we got married, and now we were investing in our growing real estate portfolio. By 1995, we'd purchased property in the Hudson Valley of upstate New York— we had restored an original 1850s farmhouse, which we then sold to our friends Scott and Dave. On the remaining thirty-four acres, we built an 8,000-square-foot, sprawling, barnlike house. It sat on a ridge and overlooked mountains and a creek with waterfalls. We fell asleep to the music of those falls whenever we spent time there. The house was beautiful, the layout designed by Jonathan and the details by me. It had a soaring stone fireplace, huge windows, and a 1,200-square-foot screened-in stone-and-cedar porch. Jonathan had a double-height painting studio built for me. It was heaven, and we felt very blessed.

To go along with our image of being among Corcoran's and New York's top-producing brokers, again with Jonathan's enthusiasm, we upgraded our clothing to designer suits and our Blazer to an Audi A8 L. It was exciting to have reached that level of success.

Then, Jonathan was told he had metastatic melanoma and three months to live, and life changed. We refused to accept the death sentence and instead agreed to believe he would be cured. We held this belief till his last breath. It was confusing to know he was sick, yet, when I looked at him, he appeared perfectly healthy. Oddly enough, it was his handsome and strong appearance that caught the attention of the second oncologist we consulted. This doctor immediately called a friend who was the head of a research team and described Jonathan in glowing terms: "I have a perfect candidate for you. He's big, strong, and handsome." He was accepted for a clinical trial that ultimately extended his life by nearly five years.

It was during this time that Alfred was offered a very lucrative position at our competitor, Douglas Elliman. As much as I wanted him to stay, I knew leaving was the best thing he could do for his career. Jonathan and I had even met with Douglas Elliman's chairman, Howard Lorber, and we both took to him immediately. This was rare for him, and Jonathan spoke of Howard often. He was excited for us to follow Alfred and also move to Douglas Elliman. But shortly after meeting with Howard, Jonathan no longer had the strength to come to the office, and I did not have the strength to make the move without him. It was sad to watch most of the brokers who sat with us on the eighteenth floor leave Corcoran to follow Alfred, who by this time had become one of the most popular managers in the city.

So Donna, Barbara, Lenny, and I moved back to the eleventh floor, where we had started at Corcoran, this time taking over Barbara Corcoran's old office. It was a lovely space that got great sunlight and had beautiful views of Central Park, and for brokers to find us, we only needed to say, "Barbara's old office." We would spend the next eight years in that office before we finally followed Alfred and our friends to Douglas Elliman.

Jonathan continued to decline. By 2008, he lived on a hospital bed in the middle of our living room, where we spent the last year and half of our lives together. Each night, I would set up an air mattress, so I could be close when he'd need me. Each morning, after helping him bathe, I would make tea with honey and raisin-walnut toast with jam. Sitting together to sip and talk and pray was a part of the rhythm and ritual of our days. One morning the phone rang, and it was Paul.

Paul's wife, Annemarie, was fighting metastatic breast cancer. A friend of a friend thought that all four of us should talk and have our own spiritual support group. We talked about strength and encouraged one another not to give up. Jonathan and I never talked about the possibility he might die and neither did Paul and Annemarie. After we hung up from that initial call, Jonathan said, "He's a really good man." Six months later, Annemarie died. Eleven days later, Jonathan died. Jonathan's battle had been long and difficult, though not without its extraordinary intimacy and miracles. Annemarie was gone as quickly as a flower blooms, fading from the day she was diagnosed.

Alfred had been with me when I was waiting for the undertaker to come for my husband's body and trying to decide how to handle his remains. I was dreading the process of the next few days which I knew I did not have the energy for. Jonathan had had a long battle and I desperately needed time to heal from physical exhaustion and especially from the loss of the beautiful man who was the love of my life for twenty-eight years and my partner in all things real estate.

"Joanne, you have been in this struggle for six years," Alfred said. "You took care of Jonathan around the clock for the past eighteen months while he was on that bed. It's time to go Italy."

Even though I had grown up in a Catholic environment of wakes and funerals, I much preferred the way my Jewish friends buried their dead. Following the funeral, everyone would come to your home to pay their respects. Instead of a body and piles of flowers, there'd be your friends and family and piles of food. So it was then that I decided to have a Shiva, and then go to Italy.

The entire real estate industry showed up, hundreds coming through my home, including the owners of each of the companies

Jonathan and I had been with: Diane Ramirez of Halstead; Barbara Corcoran with Scott Durkin, who had been Barbara's chief operating officer, and whom everyone thought would one day fill Barbara's shoes; Pam Liebman, the woman who did become CEO and president of Corcoran when Barbara sold her company; and Howard Lorber, the man who would eventually make my move to Douglas Elliman as easy as possible.

Ten days after the Shiva, Alfred, Donna, and I were in Florence. I realize now that this is how the Renna family copes: we go somewhere; we keep on living, eating, and, if we can, laughing. It doesn't mean we are not also grieving.

A few days into our trip, as we three sat at a café in the sun of a beautiful mountaintop town, I watched an aged couple, linked arm in arm, stroll past us. I turned back to my family, my heart heavy knowing I would not share the beauty of that time of life with Jonathan. I thought of my parents, Millie and Al, who were still alive and very much in love. Then Alfred raised his wineglass and said, "L'chaim," the Hebrew word meaning "to life." We clinked glasses and chimed together, "L'chaim" and christened our healing voyage the "L'chaim Tour."

Since our parents were getting on in years, at least one of us stayed behind when we traveled. This time Rosemary and our nephew, Rico, manned the home front while the rest of us cried, ate, drank, shopped, and, most especially, laughed our way through the grief.

We ended our European travels in Copenhagen, where we were so inspired by the simplicity of Nordic design that I came back with an extra suitcase filled with thick sheepskin and lots of rough wool and linen, items that a few years later became a popular design esthetic that has its roots in midcentury modern.

Two days after our return to New York, I jumped on a plane to visit friends in California. After that, Rosemary, Rico, and I drove down to Richmond, Virginia, to spend New Year's Eve with friends.

When I stopped traveling, I crashed. Then Paul called. Two days later, he called a second time. Five minutes later, he called again to ask if he could call me the next evening and read to me as he had read to Annemarie. We spoke for thirty-nine nights in a row, falling in love and grieving together. It was intense and very crazy. I'd sleep for two hours and then head to the office in a fog. Thankfully, Donna and Lenny took over everyday business. On the fortieth day, Paul arrived in New York City for what would be the only blind date either of us had ever been on. Before then, we didn't even know what each other looked like. A few family dinners and Paul was embraced by every Renna. It didn't hurt that he can build anything and has a booming Texas laugh.

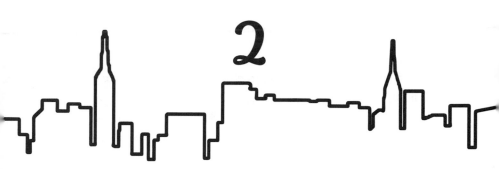

Power Brokers Conquer the Mountain

The internet changed the model of most every business, and for us, it was amazing. Corcoran's award-winning website was the most important tool for the individual salesperson to grow into a power broker. Their stunning web presence was a spotlight on the company's branding; cutting-edge technology became crucial to drawing the best agents.

In 2000, Jonathan and I had made the difficult decision to move to Corcoran. At the time, I had been working at Halstead with its owners Clark Halstead and Diane Ramirez. We had loved our time with Halstead and had grown quite close to Clark and Diane. I cried while I tried to tell Diane we were leaving. Less than a year later, on September 11, 2001, New York City suffered one of the most devastating attacks on US soil. Surprisingly, three months later, we entered the hottest real estate market the city had seen in fifteen years. With her business growing exponentially, Barbara was concerned that her ship had become too large to handle independently, and she decided to sell. She made the stunning announcement at the annual meeting at the famous Ziegfeld Theater in Manhattan. Before she broke the news, Barbara talked about the tragedy of those two jetliners that were used as weapons against our city and its iconic Twin Towers.

I take a bit of liberty with the exact words Barbara used, but the power of her message still resonates with me today: Four of our brokers lost family members, and we have mourned with them and for all the lives that were lost. As horrible as that moment was, the country and world saw New Yorkers as a united people who came together with tremendous strength and unity not seen at any other time in history. Ironically, this show of character will also prove to be the most important marketing event for the city, because it will make everyone in the world want to be here, and this company will grow faster than I can handle. Just imagine Corcoran like a huge ship that now needs a bigger rudder, to be able to turn with the greater tides. This company now needs an owner with lots of money and the ability to help it grow.

The magic that Barbara had brought to the company slowly faded after the Corcoran Group was sold and folded into a mega conglomerate. Even the web design changed, and it seemed to reflect the heavy corporate umbrella under which it operated. Still, we would enjoy extraordinarily successful years, along with the rest of the real estate industry, under the leadership of the new CEO. All Barbara predicted came to pass.

In 2003, Howard Lorber and Dottie Herman bought Prudential Douglas Elliman, one of the oldest brokerage firms in the city. Over the years they shed the Prudential affiliation that didn't resonate in New York City as it did in the suburbs, rebuilt offices, and sought to hire the best managers in the industry. The brokers followed.

By 2014, there were more new real estate companies than ever. The competition to attract and retain talent was fierce. Howard and Dottie embarked on a quest to build the most attractive and powerful company possible, expanding into markets across the country and globe, rebranding the image of Douglas Elliman, and rebuilding their website to be reflective of beauty, light, and space. I couldn't help but think, *isn't that what we want in our homes?*

Brokers began a migration, seeking the most innovative company to be affiliated with, a company whose brand was how they saw themselves, and a company whose owners and sales managers acted as business coaches. Howard said that the broker was his customer, and so he and his managers—like Alfred—worked with people like me and my team to build sales and a dynamic business within a business.

"Unfortunately, some larger companies have lost this very vital service to their brokers," Alfred reminded me after he had moved to Douglas Elliman, while I was still at Corcoran. "In these larger companies, the managers are corporately controlled, which means they spend most of their time juggling the latest cost-cutting, managing forms and paper and sitting in meetings to brainstorm on cheap inspirational ideas to boost sales and keep people from leaving." Then he pointed out, "Finding a big pink cookie on your desk on Valentine's Day just doesn't cut it when there's no dough under the frosting."

"Alfred, it's a different business model," I countered. We were always defending our companies. It's good karma and good business to support the company you work for or with, and if the managers are keeping you motivated with fun events and birthday cupcakes, most of time, people remain delighted. However, there does come a time when we might have to analyze whether we are attaining our goals and if we have outgrown the company we are with. Job changing is big though. It can feel like having to climb Mount Everest.

"What I'm saying," Alfred persisted, "is that there are brokers who rely on a manager for real business advice, and of the many who do call me, there are some who don't even work at my company. It's why I attract talent." No matter what we sell, we all need to look at where and how to grow our own businesses, and having a manager who has the power and means to motivate and elevate our processes will add to our bottom line.

Of course, there are as many ways to build and grow a successful business as there are businesses. Take a look at the numbers of real estate salespersons and brokers for Manhattan. As of late November 2013, the borough was home to about 27,000 licensed salespersons and brokers, or 5.5 percent more than the 25,600 who were licensed at the same the prior year, according to New York State Department of State data provided to *The Real Deal*.[1] What is causing the growth? TV shows that have little to do with the reality of building a business have made real estate look like a get-rich-quick fix. Have reality real estate stars gotten rich? Yes. It is fantastic. But look behind the scenes, and you will find that these brokers work hard and smart. They learn to think creatively and entrepreneurially, are willing to take risks, and don't get discouraged. They believe that no always means maybe and that maybe is a yes.

Roughly 10 percent of real estate agents rise to the top of the mountain, and it isn't because they were all born photogenic. There is no getting away from the cameras, however, so it's worth checking online for tips on how to look fabulous in a photo, because we all can. But there's more to it than that. Some brokers have formed into mega teams to build a stronger platform or brand within their affiliated company.

At the other end of the spectrum are the lone wolves who focus on one segment of the business, such as my friend Stephano. He is one of the top individual brokers in the business, focusing solely on his core group of Brazilian buyers who want to invest in new luxury condominiums. There is also a two-man Israeli team who created a website that analyzes the market for any address you input, and in two minutes, brokers can send the info to their clients as full-blown colorful presentations with accurate numbers, charts, graphs, and all sorts of pertinent and helpful information. Others throw cocktail parties or host various events to allow their buyers and sellers to meet and to keep themselves upmost in people's minds for referrals. Newsletters, webcasts, email blasts, conventional advertising, web advertising, movie theater advertising, and social media beckon with what is for sale. Home magazines and television shows explode with the whole of real estate. All kinds of homes and a full array of ancillary industries, from design to those selling every conceivable related product, are before us in a vast display of choices. It is all a wonderful example of how ingenuity, entrepreneurship, and hard work can lead to the promise of prosperity and a life well lived.

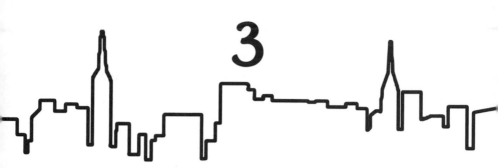

3

The Euphoria and Anguish of Sales

I took a gulp of cold water, held my hand up, and said loudly, "How many of you would like to earn five million dollars this year?" It was early in the morning, following a late martini dinner, a midnight conference call with a potential seller, and a sleepless night. I was the very last speaker of a month of intensive, full-day teachings at Corcoran's downtown learning center for new real estate agents. Every hand, even those propping up weary heads, shot up. "Okay! I'm going to tell you a story," I told the class.

Before Barbara sold our company, she'd asked me to join her to teach the secrets of real estate sales. We taught at colleges, seminars, and at Corcoran's training center. On that morning, I taught "The Euphoria and the Anguish of Sales," and boy, did I have a doozy of a story to tell.

"First, I want you all to know that I did not sleep even one wink last night because the crazy heir of a potential $50 million listing demanded a conference call at midnight!" I heard lots of murmuring:

"Oh Em Gee!"

"Fifty million?"

"Jeez."

And so I continued. "The wicked scheme of the heir was to have my team and a broker team from a different company with whom we had been competing for the listing have a debate." I let that idea settle in for moment.

For weeks, the heir would say he was about to sign the listing agreement but then demand we all meet, yet again, at 9:00 AM sharp at his late father's Manhattan penthouse, where all the floors were covered in antique limestone. He was never on time. There were days this guy would actually call while a whole team of us—including our advertising director and PR department—was already standing out in front of the famous Central Park West building to say he needed to change the meeting to 3:00 PM. And so we all had to move our schedules around and reconvene. During these meetings, he wanted to review how much money would actually be spent on promotion.

What the heir didn't know I knew was that he had recently lost all his family's money in his own ill-managed art investment fund. So he was a little bit desperate to sell the property. He had his brooding twin brother attend the numerous meetings who stared morosely at some particular spot on the Aubusson rug that was soon to go to Sotheby's auction house to help pay for the estate taxes looming ahead. I could just imagine him sticking pins in a broker doll and hexing us with warts.

Selling real estate is an amazing lifestyle. It is entrepreneurial, exciting, and challenging. It can feel psychotic, egotistical, under-handed, selfish, and thrilling, all of which creates our love-hate relationship with the business. The end of the crazy scenario with the twin heirs was that we did not get the listing, which I hated. The art investor heir had determined the asking price, adding another $10 million to what we had advised, which I loved because I figured it wouldn't sell, the listing agreement would expire, and perhaps we'd get it at a realistic asking price. I was right; it didn't sell. The price was reduced by $5 million and became a tri-exclusive listing with three different agencies. Another nine months passed, and with so many broker names on the listing—including all the partners and assistants—no one knew whom to contact for an appointment, and the second listing agreement expired. The very next day, the downstairs neighbor decided to combine apartments to create a duplex and made an all-cash offer directly to the twins. When it closed and the contract price was posted, it was for less than half of our original valuation.

Ultimately, there was another important lesson I could have shared with the twins had they been willing to listen. Unlike other parts of the country and probably the whole world, many New York City buildings have *summer work rules*. These rules exist primarily in prewar buildings, are as ancient as the buildings themselves, and are not even possible to abide by, given the additional board requirements that hundred-year-old plumbing and electric be upgraded if one is renovating. The rules say that one may renovate only during the summer when, presumably, all of your neighbors are far away in Nantucket or Kennebunkport. Now, back in those prewar days when the buildings' first fathers wrote the rules, "renovating" meant you might have been having new wallpaper put up, a gold-plated faucet installed in your powder room, or new valances hung over your windows. I've seen bylaws that still say any requests for apartment changes must be sent by telegram.

The summer time frame is impossible to stay within—no one is just hanging wallpaper or adding a few new kitchen cabinets anymore—and many buildings have instituted a daily fee that gradually increases when you pass the allocated amount of days.

Contractors add many thousands of dollars to their costs in order to follow and break the rules at the same time—along with needing a healthy budget for parking tickets, since there is virtually no legal parking for their trucks in residential zones.

There are some clever contractors who might hire a truck man, one who sits in the truck all day, driving it around the block every time the police show up. One contractor, in an attempt to get around the summer and midweek work rules—work must not begin before 9:00 AM and workers must be out of the building by 4:00 PM—had his painting crew show up in tuxedos and carrying musical instrument cases one night to give the appearance of a quartet for an after-hours dinner party. Little did the doorman know that once the quartet entered the apartment, they stripped off their tuxes, donned coveralls, and opened their instrument cases, which contained paint, painting supplies, and a boom box to play minuets. When one of the nosy neighbors rushed down to the lobby to inquire about the men in black and the music, certain the new neighbor had not yet moved in, the doorman, who had been handed an envelope of cash, assured her that the new owner was hosting an intimate dinner party with a live performance to baptize the home. Mrs. Pettitree, thus impressed, nodded with certainty and told the doorman that she had participated at the recent board interview to approve her new neighbor and "how lovely for him to support the arts. I intend to call upon him for my favorite little charity, Lincoln Center."

The twins' inherited apartment required a complete renovation, so I knew the restrictions would make the sale more complicated. The co-op board (we'll talk more about co-ops and co-op boards later) also did not allow financing, and prospective buyers would need to have at least $100 million in liquid assets, not counting the $10 million that would be needed for the renovations. It was not entirely surprising when the neighbor swooped in, getting the space for a steal.

The Incredible Kaleidoscope
of Real Estate Agents

In New York City, where there are people from every corner of the globe, agents come from every educational level, career background, country, and culture. Our diversity is rich. We've got Ivy League graduates and brilliant high school dropouts, housewives and divorcees, retirees and career changers. Each brings their own touch, cleverness, and specialty to the table.

The first group of brokers are mothers. When their kids are finally in school full-time, they turn their skills of multitasking and time management into a lucrative career. These women are vibrant, brilliant, iPhone-wielding, negotiating jugglers who have turned the PTA into a profitable field of buyers and sellers. And they sure work it. Their specialty? Young couples needing room for their growing families. They will come from PTA meetings or Pilates and manage to exude complete business composure. I did a deal on a big Park Avenue apartment with one of these lovely ladies. I was representing the buyer, an Ivy League graduate now stay-at-home mom, who happened to sit on two corporate boards and one nonprofit board, while she raised her triplets, two girls and one boy. At one of the visits to the apartment, I met the broker, Alison, who had run over from Pilates, still sweating and out of breath and wearing her black spandex. She sat on the co-op board of her own building to ensure she got the first opportunity for resales and was part of building maintenance decisions to protect property values. Without missing a single text from her nanny about one of her kid's soccer practices, she had thrown on a strand of pearls, kicked off her sneakers, and pulled ballet flats from her designer gym bag just as the buyer and her decorator arrived. And she looked gorgeous. These ladies, who can peel a banana, push a stroller, and check their emails all at once, stealthily come into the office with a specific agenda and negotiate faster than even those who hail from our next category.

The second group of brokers are former Wall Streeters who work as though they are still on Wall Street, which is a good thing. Unlike other brokers, who prefer reading the actual newspaper at home in their bathrobes till 11:00 AM, the Wall-Streeter-turned-real-estate-broker is at his or her desk in banker's suits well before the trading bell rings. Their computers are open to MSNBC to watch stock prices as they work their phones, making dozens of cold calls a day and pinging every contact they ever made. In fact, almost all of these brokers have signs over their desks to remind them of such goals, as well as their name plaque they were allowed to take when escorted out of the institution they used to work with should they have been one of the extraneous personnel of corporate downsizing or a merger. Most segue easily from selling stocks to selling homes. They are wonderful to work with because they are used to a professional environment that moves fast. Fast is good.

They document everything and save every single email. They are wizards with numbers—it's why Donna is such a successful broker. But once in a while, you get one who has a few habits from the old boys' club attitude.

We had one of these old boy Wall Streeters sitting right down the hall from our lovely corner office. His desk was in a shared windowless area, and he was flying solo—in other words, he did not have an assistant, yet he employed an old boys' network arrogance. Nevertheless, neither of us had a boss, but while attempting to consummate a sale where I represented the seller and he the buyer, he took my passing by his desk as his opportunity to give me orders.

"I encourage you to make your own copy of your buyer's financial statement if you feel the need for paper," I said to him one time. This is one example of the orders I had to throw back in his court. At first, I had visions of how to show him up or tell him off, but instead, I would go out of my way to avoid him. Then I reined in my emotions, allowed him his superiority fantasy, and shared with him any information I would share with any of my co-brokers in the mutual goal of making a sale—and my goal of getting the highest possible price for my owner. To his detriment, he dismissed everything I told him, even though we had several offers higher than his buyer's.

The seller accepted a counteroffer from a lovely couple, two professional women who trusted their broker, which meant they also trusted me, and provided everything we needed to pass the difficult board and raised their offer to meet the seller's counteroffer. Even after the contract was signed, Mr. Wall Streeter continued to demand I tell him all details of the competing buyers—which I absolutely would never do—and to inform him the moment they were turned down by the board. The ladies are happily living in their sun-filled, Beekman Place two-bedroom apartment overlooking the East River.

Occasionally, there are bad apples, and so we always keep the following in mind whether negotiating sales or life: seek to find what is good inside people and what you might offer to get positive reactions from them. As successful salespeople, we must find the key to disarm, engage, and gain the trust of the people we encounter in our businesses, whether we are negotiating with customers, colleagues, or those who provide valuable services for us.

Our next group are what Alfred refers to as "the new sexy." These are women, often referred to as being "of a certain age"—a term never used for men—who have had successful years in life whether as a career woman in a different business or from years in a real estate career. Alfred loves having these ladies around. They are intelligent, experienced, dress for success, and radiate beauty. In fact, Alfred sees them as the French do their women, sexy and able at any age. It's a new way of thinking in an atmosphere that primarily promotes youth.

The Millennials are the new kids on the block. The mature brokers watch, from the corner of their eyes, how these younger agents conduct their business. This group looks at real estate as a viable career right out of school and treats it as a tech-based business, even though it is also a multigenerational industry with no retirement requirement and has systems of doing business that have not changed in decades. You can see the difference in the desks. A Millennial's desk is often empty, as though they never moved in. They want everything to work through apps and texts and are frustrated when they have to step outside their world and use what they see as antiquated, like paper, or having to make a person-to-person phone call. They're eager to learn the business and expect everything to be instant, including having their own PR agent.

"I have to tell them to start working renters and first-time buyers, and get experience actually doing business before they hire a publicist," Alfred once explained. "They're disappointed when they learn that their careers are not as instant as gathering friends and followers on social media. Yet they are the fastest-growing generation of our business and see themselves as entrepreneurs, and we love this about them."

Alfred describes the most successful Millennial in his office as an old soul. "The Millennials, such as one of my youngest agents, Jordan, see their parents' circle of influence as their own. To cut her teeth, Jordan first tapped into her Facebook friends who needed cheap rentals." After a few successful leases were signed, she branched out, learning very quickly how to bridge the gap from her generation to her parents' generation, using all forms of communication, including the old-fashioned landline telephone. "Now this is a young woman who carries herself in a very mature manner, and she established her next goal: to build her business and gain the trust of at least one of her parent's friends." He listened in as she made her first call. It was to one of her father's law firm partners, whom she had heard was looking to purchase in a new condo development as an investment. "She was very direct and asked if she could treat him to coffee and present a few ideas." Of course, knowing her since she was a child, he was tickled and said yes. She brought along full-blown flow charts of previous sales' histories and rental incomes along with projections of future incomes and increasing values of condominiums, all presented on her iPad and subsequently forwarded to him. No doubt Jordan had an advantage in having known him so long, but she still had to prove herself and she did so with flying colors. He dismissed the broker he'd been working with who had years of experience but who had not given him any market analysis. Further, he was so impressed with her presentation that he suggested to his other partners, including her father, that they consider investing in one-bedroom condominiums as rental properties. And, as she had included in her pitch, she already had a stream of potential tenants. In less than a year, Jordan had nearly a million dollars in gross commissions on the books.

She knew her audience, and not only did she know how to reach them, but she also knew how to connect them. This young agent, who grew up on apps and social media, is under thirty, works alone, and, most importantly, puts in long hours working hard.

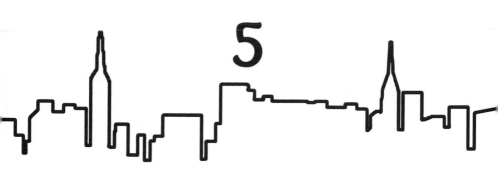

5

The Negotiator: How Alfred Began His Real Estate Career

Alfred and I were sitting at my kitchen table in the city, talking about how much we still loved being in real estate. We had actually started within months of each other, back in the '80s; Alfred reminded me that he was first and of how he had begun his career:

My first job in real estate was in 1984 selling co-ops and condos for a company called Phase II in Floral Park, Queens. Since it was commission only, I took a job as a taxicab driver with Ollie's cab service in Little Neck, where we had grown up. I figured I'd work the morning shift and sell real estate in the afternoon. I began and ended my taxi career in one day. I just couldn't relate to the dispatcher, who was burly and rough and liked to belittle the drivers, most particularly those who dared to read in his presence. Reading was a big joke to this guy, and he especially made fun of one of driver who was reading *To Kill a Mockingbird* while awaiting calls for riders. I remember that because Harper Lee lived in Rosemary's building.

I drove some kids to school, some old folks to a nursing home, took a few shoppers to the stores. I had to learn the radio lingo, a language in and of itself. I was fluent in the first two hours. After my very first four-hour shift, I took the car back to the station, turned in the keys, and I resigned. It took one shift to motivate me to sell those co-ops and con-dos as fast as I could.

At this point I figured, let me get some sales under my belt and bring my experience to the big city. In six months, I sold ten properties and became the top sales agent in the office. Once I got the hang of it, it was like selling candy. I quickly learned that if you painted a picture for buyers, of how they might live in a particular space, they couldn't resist. For example, I would show them where they might have a café table and two really comfortable chairs. "Imag-ine yourselves sitting right here in your robes, sipping your morning coffee, and reading the paper together." Then one day while driving down Jericho Turnpike I said to myself, *What the heck am I doing here? Manhattan is so close, it's time to cross the river.* Plus, Rosemary was getting ready to move full-time to the Hamptons, and I was able to take over her apartment in the city.

It was 1985, and I ended up at L.B. Kaye. At the time, it was the most advanced real estate company in the city. They had contemporary ideas in office design and how they set up their business. My other career choice had been banking. Our father's very good friend already had a position for me with the international bank he was president of. I had met with several of his upper level underlings there, but it was too narrow, stiff, and regimented.

In 1978, I spent spring semester of college in Rome that changed everything. To be exposed to so much beauty in architecture and design, and to people with amazing talents which they turned into great careers, inspired me to be creative and entrepreneurial. I had always been fascinated by how houses are built and communities develop around industry, and the history of growth of this ancient city was amazing. The area of Trastevere, as just one example, had been home, first to the Etruscans, then to Jews and Syrians who fished the Tiber. Their cottage-like houses were tiny and close together on the narrow cobblestone streets that wound up from the banks of the river. As Rome grew, and a new stone bridge replaced the wooden one, crossing the Tiber with horse drawn carriages became possible, and the rich merchants of Rome began to build villas in Trastevere, grand opulent architecture right beside the small modest working class homes. While I was not on track to be an architect, the seeds were planted that would eventually lead to my career in real estate, but not before three years of trying out various other entrepreneurial endeavors. In fact, the idea for pantomiming to help my real estate customers envision the possibilities of a home came from a very animated class I took with the famous movie director Lina Wertmuller. The unfortunate sale of our family summer home in Sag Harbor while I was abroad, informed through a shocking letter from my mother, had also motivated me to consider real estate as an alternative career option, and to earn the money to eventually replace the great loss of a summer house for myself. On my return to my schooling in the States during my last semester, I had immediately signed up for a real estate law class. This had qualified me for the required hours of education for the New York State sales license.

By 1991, after six years with L.B. Kaye, I was thinking about a different track within real estate. Instead of being a traditional real estate agent, I began selling conversions—when a rental building converts to condominium or cooperative, the sponsor, or owner of the building, will have warehoused units to be sold on the open market rather than to those insiders who were renters and had the option to purchase their own units. My on-site experience for L.B. Kaye got me noticed by Barbara Corcoran, founder of the Corcoran Group. I was ready to make a move, and Barbara wanted me to work on-site at a building where the sponsor had lost control to the bank that held the mortgage. This had followed one of the financial crises in the economy that caused a long dip in the real estate market. Virtually all the agents this job was offered to, who were already with Corcoran, had turned it down, because the base salary was too low at $12,000 a year. When I accepted the position, it was the potential commissions and not the salary that I focused on.

We had a one-year contract to sell all of the empty units. Barbara priced the same-sized apartments at the same number regardless of condition, layout, floor, position in building, or view. All the studios were the same price, all the one bedrooms were the same price, and all the two bedrooms were the same price. My gut told me this would be successful, only it didn't tell me how successful.

We used only word of mouth to market the opening day of the sale. When I showed up the first morning at the sales office on the ground floor of the building, I had to make my way through a barrage of buyers and brokers waiting for us to open. Stacey was my sales partner, and I was meeting her for the first time that Saturday morning. We were overwhelmed by the number of people waiting to get in. What was expected to take one year, took barely one weekend. In fact, it was sixteen hours of chaos with buyers flying from unit to unit like crazy people. I'll never forget one lady who was nine months pregnant, running down the hall in her high heels, screaming, and waving her contract. By Sunday morning, the buyers were afraid to take the time to even look at the apartment they were interested in, knowing in those few precious moments, they would lose it. By the end of the day, we had a stack of signed contracts sky high. Every single unit sold. It was the commissions from these sales that enabled me to buy my first piece of property, my house in Southampton, now valued at more than ten times what I paid for it.

This sales event with Barbara became known, throughout the Manhattan real estate industry, as the famous one-day sale, changing the lives of everyone involved. I had made so much money, I was ready to go live in Europe for a year or so when I received a phone call with an offer I couldn't refuse, as it was from a well-known property-owner and major landlord for a great salary with bonuses based on my success. It was to be the negotiator. The position would also be an area of interesting experience to add to my real estate resume. Off I went to renegotiate leases for a man who owned thousands of apartments.

Nine months later, Barbara wanted me back, this time as a sales manager. Another offer too good to pass up, and I returned to continue to build her west side gallery into a profitable office. Then one day, she called with an invitation for breakfast. I figured it had to be for good reason because why else would she want to have breakfast with me. We met at the Regency at 7:00 AM. She said, "Alfred, I've been watching you for the past year. I like how your mind works, the questions you ask, your interest in all the departments, and how well you get along with everyone. You are the perfect candidate to take Corcoran into the twenty-first century."

I had to ask her what that meant.

"Technology and the internet," she answered, which I knew nothing about.

But I accepted the challenge and she immediately had me start classes at Columbia University for computer science. As soon as I had some understanding of the way computers worked, I moved to the corporate office and created new technology systems for all the sales offices, replacing all the computers, screens, wiring, equipment, and especially the platform from which the sales agents worked. Then came the biggest challenge. I put together a team and designed and built what would become an award-winning website. It was the first to identify and support the change in online business that I was able to document. This was huge. In fact, this achievement was recognized by Microsoft which used my reporting to support their belief in how the internet was going to change business. It certainly changed Corcoran by putting more selling power in the hands of the broker.

For our first website design, Barbara had given me one directive. She said, "I do not want my photograph anywhere on the website." But she turned down every design and mockup I did. She hated layout after layout. Our home page had to be exceedingly special.

Then, in spite of what she told me, I had a thought to go ahead and do a layout featuring her in one of the dozen red suits she always wore. We had lots of photos to use as her image was on some of our ads and brochures. Before I showed it to her, I had a little editing done after having seen a documentary on how fashion magazines changed photos, enhancing the models. So I figured, fashion model? Why not Barbara Corcoran. I made her legs the equivalent of a foot longer, and did a bit of reshaping. She was a knockout. I waited for the right moment to present it. Late that day, I walked into her office with the layout on a big board facing her. She took one look and said, "Wow! I look great! Let's do it!" I left the office laughing, and she called me back to ask what was so funny.

I said, "You're going to kill me." I was still laughing and could barely get the words out to say to her, "Those aren't your legs."

She laughed with me and said, "No wonder I love it!" Corcoran.com became a national leading website.

After this great success, my core team and I were assigned new office space. When Barbara called me in to tell me about it, I was very excited. That was until I looked at the blueprint of the newly expanded office space that was undergoing a complete *build-out*, the term used for office renovations. To my great disappointed, I saw we were right in the middle of the entire office, far from the wonderful huge windows in what would clearly be a small, sunless, shared space with tiny desks. Nothing special or rewarding given the success of my project. I was not about to whine and complain, and knowing how much she appreciates humor, I decided to thank her with a photo illustrating my interpretation of our newly assigned stations.

I took Sheldon, Julie, and myself into the men's bathroom. We staged one of the bathroom stalls as a private office. I had a small file cabinet brought in to act as the desk, balancing an old computer monitor, mouse, and phone on top. Then we each took turns sitting on the toilet with a keyboard on our lap to take photos. I then created a triptych of the three of us with big smiles, gleaming with joy and appreciation. I wrote a note on the photo that said, "Dear Barb, Thank you for our new private offices. Love, Alfred, Sheldon, and Julie. I printed it and put it on her desk. As soon as she saw it, she called me into her office. She was laughing so hard she nearly peed in her pants.

"Alfred, this goes into my special file of things I keep forever." Shortly thereafter, each of us were awarded a private windowed office, and I got to design my own furniture.

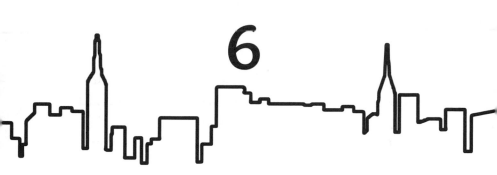

6

The Tenaciousness
of Social Agents

Our industry has a history of attracting women who enter the business after having reached a certain time in their lives. Some do so because they love being social and real estate is an excellent place to utilize their society contacts. Others are empty-nesters and looking to make a new and meaningful contribution to the community. Some are divorcees who have never worked and find they have to.

"These ladies are tenacious once the last alimony check has been spent. I can tell by the increased frequency to my office," Alfred said. He really enjoys working with these women and recognizes the value of their life experiences—lunching, socializing, fundraising, and managing school committees—and turning them into a lucrative career. These are often women of a generation who left finances entirely to their successful husbands. The fact that they became accustomed to a certain way of living adds to their hunger for success.

"Jeanette, one of the intelligent and beautiful ladies who works with me, had been having a tough time getting her business started," Alfred told me. Apparently, she was embarrassed by her lack of computer knowledge and waited to ask for help until she was even having difficulty sending and receiving emails. "After sitting and getting comfortable, she leaned forward and whispered, 'I need more memory. Alfred, how do I get more memory? Do you have to approve that?' So I told her that we all would like more memory, but she certainly did not need my approval." He laughed as he told me the story. "I told her: Jeanette, you're not getting emails because you now have thirty-six thousand of them. You're supposed to delete them after you've read them, except for those that need to go into a separate file for a deal, as we have our own server with a limited memory. She didn't know she had to delete emails."

While that may seem ignorant of basic business at that time, Alfred knew that, with tech help and coaching, he could turn her into a powerful broker. She had a need and a desire for her own income. She had received the marital apartment free and clear plus her ex-husband's entire mailing list that she managed—friends, acquaintances, and everyone they had ever met. So when Alfred saw she had no contacts on her Outlook, he asked her about it. That's when she pulled from her Hermès Birkin bag a thick address book, every entry in her perfect penmanship, and chock-full of potential customers. He immediately had one of the staff members enter them into her Outlook contacts and show her how to print out mailing labels.

"I told her to write a quarterly newsletter, and she came up with the idea of including copies of her favorite recipes, courtesy of a complete collection of the Barefoot Contessa cookbooks her former husband had once given her." The calls started to come in. Now her visits to Alfred's office are to strategize negotiations and pitching new exclusives. He's even found a perfect assistant and broker event escort for her.

The "ladies who lunch" are a social group who don't need to work. Imagine a woman in sensible Tory Burch pumps that could make a certain kind of leg look shorter, though not the long, thin limbs of these socialites, who dine on undressed romaine lettuce and black coffee while wearing bouclé-knit Chanel suits in pastel colors accessorized with tasteful jewelry. These ladies are doyennes from the old-school of selling prewar co-ops with a well-placed whisper at cocktails or bridge. If a divorce or death is imminent, a wonderful Park Avenue home could quietly find its next owner. We barely have a handful of these powdered ladies left, as so many have left the business—but not before having gifted others the secrets to passing the most difficult of co-op boards.

I used to have the European version of one of these ladies on my team. Nina was the doyenne of doyennes. Her accessories of choice were a cloud of perfume, pounds of jangling gold, and yards of extravagant scarves. She would hold court by sharing extraordinary secrets of famous stars and various world leaders—including one of our most beloved presidents—and discussing the merits of the Democratic party and the latest debate she had with her very Republican husband. Unlike her contemporaries, Nina worked hard in real estate and was proud of the successes she enjoyed.

These ladies have utilized their sphere of influence to solicit and quietly conduct business in the trifecta of New York high society: the Upper East Side, Southampton, and Palm Beach.

We've also got a group we refer to as "the knitters." They come to the office to schmooze. The office is their social network. They will walk about, peering over reading glasses, their perfume preceding them, seeking people they can kibitz with, and give you the latest chapter of their successful children's lives—and myriad details of their grandchildren, should they have any.

The ones who are tech savvy will show you photos on their smartphones, but mostly they will be seeking information to knit together: the latest divorce or other scandal, what competitors are offering, who's left which company for another. They will talk about other brokers all day, especially who had the latest facelift. The way the doyennes know Park Avenue boards, the knitters know when the best sales are coming up at the three Bs (also known as the famous New York stores: Bloomingdale's, Barneys, and Bergdorf's), who is holding a sample sale, and where you can buy Cartier watches at a discount. They also know the best cleaning ladies, can find a nanny better than any agency, and have contacts at all the private schools. Their most important job is to dispense unsolicited advice about life.

"So when . . . ?" Donna was asked a couple of years ago, when she first met Michael. The intonation and properly elongated "when" translates to: "When are you getting married to that schlemiel already?" Within days of a honeymoon, the follow-up "So when . . . ?" means: "When are you two having children?" Which really means, you're getting old, your eggs are getting old, and you must do your part to contribute to filling the earth already.

Alfred is often approached by his knitters, no matter if it's at the office about to enter the men's room or at the pricy specialty food shop Citarella's with a similar "Sooooo?" This covers all things not covered by "So when?" It is also the signal that they intend on keeping you for as long as necessary.

"As managers," he offered with raised eyebrows, "we allow for their monopolizing our time and their mild complaining in order to be one of the first beneficiaries of their insider information." Real estate fodder and any gossip that will eventually lead to the selling or buying of real estate is their greatest contribution, and we all appreciate their investigative skills. Not surprisingly, if these ladies do snare an exclusive listing, they are never available to show when other agents request a time. Also, these ladies—they are never men—

always want you to call them the morning of the appointment you have already confirmed to reconfirm.

"I can tell you, if and when they have a deal, there is always trouble. Into my office they march, as having a good listing is empowering. This is called the power of the listing through which they have elevated their own importance." Alfred said, "We all allow them their idiosyncrasies." He did finally have to move one recently to a former utility closet, as she required that no other agent sitting near her wear perfume, complaining that no one's fragrance was as well chosen as her own. But we love our stiffly-coifed and well-scented women, with their clanking bangles and charm bracelets, who bless us with life wisdom, believing all that they do is for the betterment of mankind— and in our world, it is.

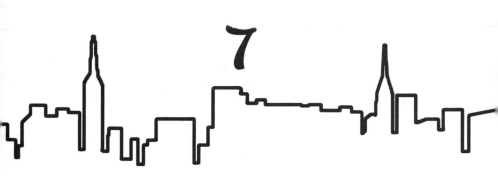

7

The Rennas Negotiate
New York

We Rennas are our very own category of broker. Why? It's not because we like to think we are lucky, though other people tell us that all the time. There are a couple of other family teams, mostly husbands and wives or parents and children. There are those siblings out there who quarrel all their lives and end up living as far away from each other as possible. But we Rennas—we quarrel but still stick together. As life has changed, our careers have transformed. In 2016, Donna and I finally moved to Douglas Elliman. Rosemary was the last to join in on all the fun, forgoing her trip to visit her properties in Italy to help get The Douglas Team organized. The four of us Rennas literally have our offices on the same floor—Donna, Rosemary and I, continuing as The Douglas Team from when Jonathan and I were working together and how we are known to our longtime customers, and Alfred who is an executive manager of Elliman. It was one of the requests I made to Howard, that our office was near Alfred's, and he agreed. Laughing and having fun are keys to balanced and healthy working relationships, especially for us, as we spend most of the workweek together in the city, marketing real estate, and then spend weekends together in the Hamptons, purchasing, building, and decorating our own real estate. We work hard, but at least once a day, after hours, Donna, Rosemary, or I might say, "Let's take a design break." It's our version of going outside for a cigarette. One of us will pull up a fabulous coffee table we've been considering, and we'll crowd around their computer screen for a look and design input. At rare moments, Alfred pops into our office to show us a photo of the latest lamps he's bidding on from Chairish.com.

We get lots of visitors to our office, friends and colleagues who just like to visit. At business events, it's kind of like being quadruplets, as we four siblings stick together, work together, and laugh together. And we also have our many "adopted" siblings, those friends who love to laugh, are supportive, and know the powerful allure of all things real estate and family, not necessarily in that order!

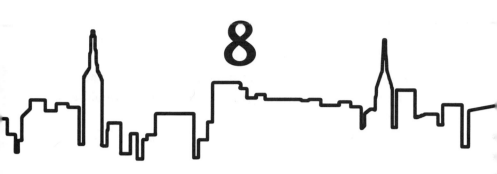

8

Partners, Teams, and Tribes

Lots of brokers like to work in groups. It could be because they are family members or perhaps are drawn together by shared interests or past careers—dog lovers, former decorators, a gaggle of models, and so on. Others come together because they share the same cultural background. The Douglas Team is a prime example of both. Donna and I are partners and we are sisters, but we have a growing team of mixed backgrounds where each member is creative. I'm a writer; Donna, a photographer; Barbara, a portrait artist; Rosemary, a decorator; and Lenny, a cityscape artist. And we all have our extended and overlapping circles of friends, hailing from all ethnicities and proclivities.

A few years ago, I had a fantastic penthouse listing on Fifth Avenue. A broker new to the United States, from Israel, and also new to brokerage made an appointment with me to show his new buyer this home. Adept at appointment overlapping, he had warned me that he had not yet met his buyer and that, unfortunately, he would be coming from another appointment. He asked if I would please show her around and keep her there till he showed up.

I slowly walked the woman around the three-bedroom duplex, saving the beautiful outdoor space for last. I had told the doorman to send the broker straight up and that I'd leave the door unlocked for him. This practice is not unusual when showing apartments in New York City, and in fact, many co-op owners never lock their doors. No one gets past our doormen without them knowing who the people are. I could smell Mosha's hypnotic cologne before he stepped out to the terrace. His wealthy buyer was leaning on the railing, causing her short designer dress to pull up, exposing more of her very long, tanned legs. This did not go unnoticed by Mosha. As I introduced them, I could not stop the fifteen-year-old side of my brain from saying to the adult side: *Would you trade your face for those legs?* Mosha snapped his phone closed and poured out his charm, taking her extended hand, not to shake it, but to put it to his lips. As he released it, he ran his hand through his thick hair, showing off a bicep as well formed as her calves and easily seen beneath his perfectly tailored jacket sleeve.

He swept her out of the apartment as he called the next broker to beg their forgiveness for being tardy, and asked would they please wait as he had the perfect buyer for their listing.

Another brilliant group with thousands of centuries of negotiating skills behind them is the Chinese. The best of the best of our Chinese brokers will start negotiating with you long before their buyer steps over the threshold of a potential property, and the negotiating does not stop at contract signing. I witnessed one of their exceptional sales talents when, at a closing, I represented the seller and my colleague the buyer. She and I sat at the far end of the conference table where she quickly informed me that she had already sold her buyer a better listing that had just come on the market that week, and that she would be selling the apartment about to close, for a profit. One more point to note is that Chinese brokers have an abacus in their brain and can calculate their commission faster than you can press your cell's send button. They can also be charming, beautiful, and fun.

One of my favorite real estate sales experiences was with a vivacious Greek broker. The Greeks like to stick together. We know because our Greek friends like to tell us as much. They have clans within the greater clan. Most importantly, they have a vast network of potential business within their community, and Greeks like to work with Greeks.

This particular broker had, as a buyer, a very important Greek person, and all involved did their homework. There was a front team made up of imposing VIPs with strong voices, personalities, and opinions. The team arrived first to preview the eight-room listing that had just been renovated. It was an Upper West Side condominium, with wall-to-wall windows and disappointingly low ceilings that were countered by spectacular Hudson River views. After a private huddle in the living room, it was apparent this elite posse was to determine which homes their leader would view and that my listing would be the apartment at the top of the list.

A week later, the prospective resident arrived with his entourage. He was humble, soft-spoken, and had a long beard. He wore simple, black clothing and a rather large cross hung around his neck. His team, who preceded him from the elevator to the open front door where I stood, bowed and walked backward as if lying down palm fronds for his arrival. They all exuded such honor to be in this man's presence. He quietly asked to be left alone with me to have a tour. The entourage retired to another room as he took my arm with his soft hand. I fell in love with this special man in a single moment. He radiated love, peace, patience, and wisdom of the ages. He took slow, deliberate steps, and he leaned his head toward mine to speak softly about the qualities of the apartment, which room might be best for his study, did I think it would be okay for him to take one of the smaller bedrooms, which he would prefer, which bedroom would be most comfortable for his personal cook, and so on. I didn't want our time to end. But his group was anxiously awaiting his reaction, standing in a tight circle, in the farthest, smallest room, which was set off from the living room and held only an old TV and small love seat. The special gentleman nodded with approval to each of us, then smiled as if to sanctify us all.

Afterward, I researched who he was on Google and learned he was in fact almost as well-known for his teachings of peace around the world as the Dalai Lama. My listing was purchased for him to live in while in New York, and I know his prayers bless our rivers, roadways, subways, skyscrapers, boroughs, and all of us who make this city our home, whether for a brief time or for life.

Another very specialized group is the retired men. To their credit, they find working is more interesting than actual retirement, and with their years of business contacts, real estate is a natural segue. Some of these successful career men might go solo, but it seems most join their wives to form husband-and-wife teams. Much of the time, the man is following in the footsteps of his power broker wife, essentially becoming her assistant until he is up to speed. "Yes, there is some resistance," Alfred offers with a firm nod. "Those coming from high-powered, authoritative corporate positions, such as advertising, have a tough time seeing brokerage as a real career. That usually ends when he starts to see what it takes to be a successful broker." And so, as an apprentice, he's there to assist, learn, tag along, and escort his wife. Escorting seems to be his favorite job duty, as it plays into his experience of golf outings, private club lunches, and other social events where contacts and deals are made.

You always see these new junior agents accompanying their wives to all the best open houses, cocktail parties, and the annual antique show at the Park Avenue Armory. Their ties tell you either their former profession or university, and they have hearty laughs. They talk a lot about their latest golf outing.

Each year, Donna and I are invited to the opening night of the Park Avenue antiques show. It is an industry-related event by virtue of one of the sponsors, Chubb, the best insurance company in the industry and where we send our clients. As we circle up and down the rows of priceless antiquities, we people watch, as does everyone else. One year, we heard a rare antiques dealer engaged in conversation about some extraordinary piece he was hoping to sell. Standing within easy refill distance to the bar was a circle of blue sports jackets, khaki pants, bow ties, a few potbellies, and clinking glasses of bourbon on the rocks. These husbands, each anointed with new real estate licenses, were discussing those things that such clans discuss—articles they read in the *Wall Street Journal* that morning, their last golf score, and the size of their successful wife's shoe collection.

In the mix, there was one younger broker who had joined his successful mother's team and, despite his law degree from NYU, was also considered an apprentice. These young men, such as their retired elder counterparts, are great junior brokers and escort their mothers to all sorts of fun broker events. Their dress style is the same private school uniform that all men, young or old, of a certain group are loathe to ever give up.

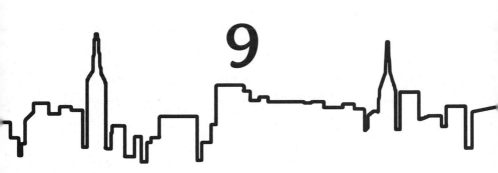

9

Friends, Shoes, and Real Estate

We all have our circles of influence that were seeded in real estate, the foundation to many great alliances, from friendships to marriages. In my case, a long-lasting book club and many wonderful friendships were born out of the sale of a great loft. In fact, the real estate genetics of the book club go back even further, to when I was a young, single woman in the city and had a roommate with a friend who needed a place to crash when he was in town for acting classes. This was in 1983. When my first roommate moved out, her friend the cute actor, Dennis, continued to show up every Tuesday night, and I continued to allow him to sleep on the living room floor. The only furniture I could afford at the time was my bed, but the floor in New York City was prime real estate for the young and striving.

I, myself, a low-salaried fashion designer working for a garment manufacturer supplying stores like Sears and JC Penney, was in the midst of searching for a new roommate who could pay half the rent, which in turn would enable me to buy a pair of shoes I had to have. Right at that time, a friend of Alfred's who had been working in LA was looking for an apartment to share for her move back to New York City. I soon had my second real roommate and a new pair of fabulous red, woven-leather Bottega Veneta high-heeled pumps. Days after Janet moved in, she met Dennis, our weekly visitor. A year later, they married and moved to their own apartment. First they lived Downtown, then Uptown, then down to Miami, and finally, a few years later, back to New York. The best payback for a free place to crash, albeit twenty-five years later, was that the actor had given my name to an acquaintance of his who was looking for a broker. That's how I met Loretta.

The first day out touring Chelsea, Loretta and I discovered we had the same interests. We had so much fun getting to know each other while looking at properties, and we reacted the same way to everything, smiling, smirking, and rolling our eyes. We loved the same things—great art, design, architectural potential, and shoes. Then we got into talking about food, wine, purses, and books. Following the first rounds of look sees, Loretta brought her husband, Simon, to the best lofts we had previewed. They purchased one and spent nine months renovating; then they threw a wonderful move-in party. In the midst of the revelry around us, Loretta stopped to ask me, "How would you like to join a new book club that Kerry (her architect) and I are starting?"

This was during Jonathan's illness, and despite the challenges we were faced with, he still encouraged me to join. Book club nights were the only times during his illness that I went more than a block from the apartment. The book club became a refuge; our little group was a great support for all of us.

We are five women: Loretta is the quick-witted girl from Queens who grew up working in the warehouse of her family's auto parts business. She married her opposite, Simon, a soft-spoken Englishman and Cambridge scholar. When their two boys were just about out of the house, Loretta unexpectedly became an heiress when a large company approached her family about buying their business. She now generously contributes to our community, donating her intelligence and time to Doctors Without Borders, and our museums, MoMA and the Met, as well as collecting fabulous shoes, purses, and art and always looking glamorous and sexy.

Ilsa is married to Jabin Stein, and they are always full of energy. They are both also intelligent and fabulous conversationalists. One could easily imagine them the king and queen of the prom. Ilsa teaches high school students English as a second language, and Jabin, an accountant, is the CFO of a commercial window supplier and loves anything that has to do with building and renovating.

Then there is Marisola, the sizzling lady from Spain. Half the time she hasn't finished the book, as she is always busy traveling, whether taking care of someone or out West, skiing, but we don't have any rules except to eat, drink, and have a good time. When we started our club, she was married to an investment banker, Ted.

And of course, there is Kerry, who helped initiate the club and is married to architect, Reed. They are both tall, attractive, smart modernists who live in a prewar apartment.

Things none of us could ever have fathomed were revealed each month as our lives unfolded along with the fictional lives of the characters in the novels we read. We would discuss the book, and then we would discuss our lives. My book club sisters mourned with me when my husband died. Three months later, they happily shared in the stories of my phone calls with Paul without judgment that too little time had passed. My story became like a series, the ladies waiting for the next installment. One night, Loretta exclaimed, "This is better than the book!" Then, they shared my joy when Paul and I met in person and realized that we would share our lives.

The men started their own club, ironically referring to themselves as the Illiterates and meeting at restaurants while we ladies held our book club nights in each other's homes. By the time the men started the Illiterates, we had one deceased husband, one gay soon-to-be ex-husband, one architect, one scholar and wine connoisseur, and, of course, the cowboy from Texas who went from rounding up cattle on his grandfather's ranch to climbing oil rigs, to building high-end condos in Dallas. Paul was a perfect fit.

Four years had passed since the inception of our club when my former roommates and Alfred's friends Janet and Dennis were visiting New York City and arguing on West Ninety-Sixth Street. Ted and Marisola, pre-divorce and looking like the perfect Hollywood couple in their convertible, pulled up to say hi. Despite what seemed like an embarrassing moment, they reconnected and had dinner together. That's when Janet said to Marisola, "We're moving back to New York, and I want to find a book club to join."

None of us ever wanted to upset the carefully curated group, but it seemed meant to be. I said Janet would be a perfect fit, we all said yes, and the men welcomed Dennis to their dinners. Since the very beginning, there have been lots of real estate goings-on— one of the most exciting was Simon and Loretta buying a house in Southampton. We have also had our share of real estate casualties. After thirty-four years of marriage, Ted and Marisola called it quits. No amount of therapy was going to make a marriage between a beautiful, hot-blooded woman and a gay man with fabulous clothes work. Their stunning Classic Seven on Riverside Drive went on the market. It was lovely to show but sad at the same time. His closets were way bigger than hers, which was not lost on the buyers who came through. Eventually, Ted and Marisola sold their Fire Island summer home as well, since sharing it wasn't going to work.

Janet immediately fit into the group, but we didn't yet know how perfectly. Months later, Loretta and I set up Alfred and Rebecca, Loretta's friend from LA, on a blind date. When Rebecca returned to LA, she was having dinner with another friend and mentioned having met a great guy named Alfred. There not being too many Alfreds in the world, Libby asked if Alfred was, by any chance, Alfred Renna. Of course it was the same Alfred. Libby screamed, "I was Janet's boss back when she was living in LA a hundred years ago. We're still best friends. I stay with her in Southampton every summer!"

"What a small world!" Alfred exclaimed when we all discovered the coincidence. And so our sixth book club member completed a thirty-five-year circle of friends, roommates, and, as Alfred said, "Real Estate. I guess you can say if it wasn't for that, all of us might have never have met."

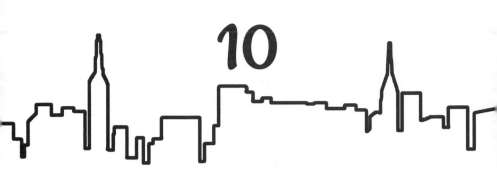

Craziest Deals: Counting Cats

One of the craziest deals I did was with Nina. Nina was my older, wise friend and teammate on The Douglas Team, who loved food. The deal was for a large penthouse apartment with a wrap-around terrace, overlooking the park. The buyers were living in LA when we saw the listing pop up on my computer. We called their financial advisor, Sheldon, to take him to preview the apartment, the price of which seemed too good to be true. The three of us ran there that same day, Sheldon with an old-fashion video camera in hand. When we got off the elevator of the elegant Central Park West building, the smell of urine hit us like a cloudburst. The listing broker had already warned us that there were a few cats in residence.

As we entered the apartment, there were not a few but *many* cats roaming in the foyer. Video camera whirring, Sheldon made his way to the first bedroom and started counting. "Seven, eight, nine. There's another—ten." His voice was now muffled by the handkerchief he held over his nose. We were in the third bedroom and up to twenty-three when his asthma caught up to him, and he ran to the terrace to breathe. Nina and I completed the video, she holding a well-perfumed handkerchief to her nose, and me with the camera, breathing as shallowly as I could. We walked carefully through waves of parting fur to cover the kitchen, staff quarters, and formal dining room and were up to forty-four before entering the living room that had a double-height ceiling. We couldn't take another breath and ran out to the terrace to join Sheldon and clear out our lungs.

"The apartment is spectacular!" we both exclaimed. Sheldon thought we were crazy. Yes, it would need to be completely gutted, but it would be worth the effort.

During negotiations, we learned that the co-op board had to sue the owner, an eccentric countess, to sell in order to get rid of the menagerie, which included four dogs of varying sizes. The only question was: When the cats were gone, could the smell of urine be eliminated? Ultimately it meant removing all of the beautiful, original floors the building was known for. It was a three-year renovation, but the apartment is now gorgeous, and I have had the pleasure of being invited to attend the annual Thanksgiving Day Parade breakfast, a favorite holiday for those fortunate enough to have homes on Central Park West with views of the park and the parade route.

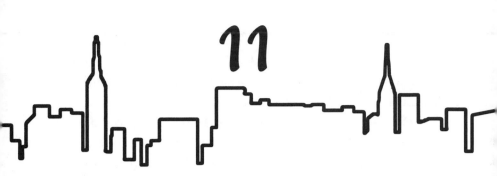

The Summer House

My three siblings and I grew up attending mass with our parents every Sunday, even out in Sag Harbor, where we spent our summers. All of us would have our swimsuits beneath our church getups, and we'd squirm in the hot pews, suppressing our uncontrollable desire to laugh, till we could run out and get to the beach as fast as possible. Our father had three brothers and a sister, and eventually all four brothers and their families owned summer homes near one another. After two summers in a rental house, our mother and father had looked to purchase land to build their own house. We kids were consulted, and it was unanimous—we were going to buy property right on the Peconic Bay. The prospect that we would have our very own beach seemed so amazing. It also gave us an education on the values of properties; waterfront would cost more money than comparable properties not on the water. To our fledgling real estate minds, this was powerful knowledge. None of us could sleep that night, we were so excited. Then, the next day, our mother blurted out her fear that one of us might drown.

After the prospect of a house on the beach was nixed, we all went to look at land in a newly developing area. We were the first interested buyers and had our choice of the one-acre, wooded parcels. The new road wound its way to the top of a hill, the highest point in the Hamptons, where we could see farmland and sun glinting off the ocean in the distance and feel its glorious breezes. Being the eldest, at twelve, I strongly advised that we buy all the lots on the road, though I was still feeling disappointed about the waterfront property. Rosemary, Alfred, and Donna all seconded the motion, though Donna was barely two at the time.

Our father wanted to build right away and told us that if we bought all that land, we would have to wait an extra year to have a house. Alfred and I can still remember thinking that it would have been worth the wait, having so much land was so strong a yearning. In time, we would have been a whole lot richer.

Our parents had taken us on several field trips for our big family project. After having chosen and gone into contract on our land, we then spent a day looking at the model homes the builder had erected somewhere "up island," as the locals would say should they venture west. There were several variations of the three- or four-bedroom layout that included a full basement, a large living room, a dining room with windows on two sides, a big kitchen, and laundry room. All the floors would be white oak, and our father insisted on bare-wood moldings around the doors and windows, with the wood grain matching. I was curious about how that would look, thinking a nice, shiny white would be nicer. I was especially excited that we would have a fireplace with a grand mantel and I really wanted to be the one making fires. After we chose our house plan and made all the decisions on finishes, we went on another, long day trip to our property. It was entirely wooded, and I loved the scent of the pines, typical of Eastern Long Island; cedars; and my favorite, white birch trees. We had orange tape to tie on the trees that we wanted the builder to keep, creating a circular driveway with islands of trees in front and in the backyard, creating both sunny and shady spots.

By the beginning of winter, before it got really cold, the foundation of our childhood summer home had been poured, and we drove out east with great anticipation to check on the progress. As we headed up the hill, our stomachs turned over and our mother started to cry—the builder had clear cut our land, from front yard to back, removing every tree and all of the rich soil that had taken hundreds of years for the forest to create. We still had the woods that surrounded the building site, but that was little conciliation while imagining the land directly around our house now barren of our beautiful trees. There were conversations of a lawsuit, but there was nothing in writing. Our father promised that we would plant lots of trees that would be even better.

By spring, the house was completed and included the basic midcentury furniture we now all wish we still had. The drive out—with two cars filled to overflowing with clothing, household stuff, kids, dog, and bird—felt like an eternity. In spite of the loss of trees that I didn't believe could be replaced, we were all excited and laughing, and piled in for the ride. Our second disappointment happened as soon as we arrived—our parents had eliminated the fireplace to save on costs, but they promised we would get one the following season. We settled into what would be the first of our wonderful childhood summers in our own house. Our parents followed the seasonal custom that was the mothers and the children would spend the whole summer out east, the fathers arriving on Thursday nights and returning to the city, and their jobs, early on Monday mornings.

It is amazing how childhood experiences inform our lives as adults. When my late husband and I bought our upstate property, we noticed blue slash marks on huge, original-growth oaks. The broker informed us they were to be cut down for lumber. I sometimes think a part of my motivation to buy that house and so much land was to save the majestic trees. The prior owner needed the money. In the offer terms, following the price, was that not a single tree be touched.

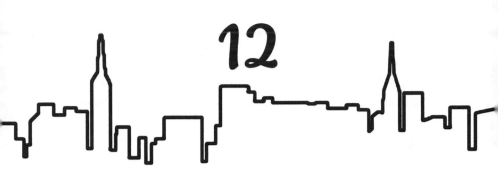

12

It's All About the
Color of Brick

The real estate market in New York City is made up of various forms of building types, materials, and architectural styles, the terms of which we might use in generic and confusing ways. We often get questions from visitors and newcomers about how it all works. For instance, when showing various types of buildings to a family from out of town, I mentioned that the first apartment I took them to was a postwar. While going up the elevator to the second apartment we were viewing, I pointed out that we were in a prewar building. Their fourteen-year-old daughter asked, "Which war?"

For building designations, we only use one war and that is World War II. Those built before are *prewar buildings*, and those built after are *postwar buildings*. Then, you have *town houses*, which are mostly single-family attached homes and usually have a small garden in back.

New Yorkers often refer to them as *brownstones* almost in a generic way. Many brownstones were built in the mid-nineteenth century of a reddish stone that had been quarried in New Jersey and Connecticut. Being nearby, it was cost efficient to bring the easy-to-cut sandstone into town on barges.

But many of the town houses in Manhattan are built from limestone and marble, which was much costlier because it had to be cut by hand and shipped in. These facades are more ornate and closer to Central Park, the "Gold Coast" of the Upper East and Upper West Sides. Town houses, which are referred to as *attached houses* or *row houses* in places like Queens and Staten Island, are priced by the foot. Every foot wider makes the property exponentially more expensive by millions of dollars. Each block you get closer to the park, the value increases.

In their heyday, these uptown mansions were built by locals, such as the Vanderbilts, Whitneys, Fricks, and New York society's wealthiest barons. By the 1920s, many of these families had sold their houses to purchase in grand apartment buildings with Otis elevators and all kinds of services. For others, the outer boroughs and suburbs beckoned. The town houses' new owners divided the buildings into rental apartments. Those rentals that maintained a full floor in a town house became known as *floor-throughs*. Young professionals would be proud to say "my floor-through" as opposed to "my apartment." Floor-throughs were romantic; they had garden and street views and fireplaces in both the living room and bedroom. Few of these apartments remain today, as town houses have reverted back to one-family homes with the cycle of newly rich barons creating a demand for space all over Manhattan. A floor-through rental hardly exists anymore.

In the 1980s, the city started to morph as the best place on all the earth to live, and single-family homes here began to look like a good investment again. The real estate brokers' advertisements rang with the desirable *delivered vacant*. A delivered vacant was a house that used to be a single-family home, or small building that could be turned into a single-family home after having been a multi-unit rental building, dormitory, or SRO. *SRO* refers to single room occupancy. You had a room with just enough space for a single bed. Tenants shared a bathroom and kitchen on the same floor. They had become popular at the turn of the nineteenth century, when affordable housing for factory workers and shop girls was needed. The option to take these buildings and convert them to single-family homes added considerable value, despite the gargantuan renovation costs.

In all cases, as you move away from the park or the heart of any of New York City's prime neighborhoods, the prices come down, the sizes decrease, the windows shrink, the details are gone, the garbage cans become prominently displayed in front, fire escapes adorn the facades, and people sit on the stoop. In Manhattan and Brooklyn, the outside steps that go up to the main door of town houses are called *stoops*. *Steps*, on the other hand, often go down to the front door of the building. One would think you would step up and stoop down, but not in Manhattan—this is just another example of things we New Yorkers do to confuse newcomers.

Back in the 1800s, when the Otis brothers got elevators up to speed and devised a safety feature that halted the cab in case the hoist rope broke, the New York City landscape began its ascent to the sky. The first apartment buildings were only six stories high because tenants didn't want to climb any higher. But after the elevator, apartment buildings were built up to twelve stories. Luxury buildings had the largest apartments on the first and second floors, where the rich would be more comfortable, being accustomed to town house living. The upper floors had smaller apartments, and the very top floors were dedicated to laundry facilities that included huge drying racks and maids' rooms. Some of the first really luxurious buildings, such as the famous Dakota and the Wyoming, were named for those western states far out in the territories, because of how far up the island of Manhattan they were built, where it was still countryside and farms.

Eventually, buildings that had been built from the late 1800s to the 1930s began to be referred to as prewar, as noted above, being prior to World War II. Following the war, the need for housing grew with the ranks of returning veterans. By the '50s and '60s, postwar building boomed. Taller, wedding-cake-style apartment buildings were going up. Wedding cake refers to the architectural design of the buildings; the higher floors had setbacks that gave the buildings a tiered-cake look and allowed sun to reach the sidewalks. It was not surprising that history led to the buildings that went up after World War II to be referred to as *postwar*. In these postwar buildings, the upper floors became more desirable and had larger units, and the top floors, which had terraces created from the setbacks, were called *penthouses*.

The prewar apartment buildings, built for and by the very rich, often had limestone facades on the first two floors, and then, from the third level to the top, they were a cream brick, all hand laid. Others were built with red brick bottom to top, except perhaps around the entry to the building, where limestone was used. Ornamental detail was evident in all fashions, from cornices to finials, and from belfries to arches and more. Postwar buildings have their own subcategories defined by the color of their brick facades. The darker the brick, the more the building could pass as a closer cousin to a prewar, the most desirable building before the newer construction. Prewar buildings have higher ceilings, more ornate detailing, and larger rooms. The postwar buildings were built with speed and cost in mind, when housing had suddenly been scarce. For many years, white postwar buildings were less desirable than red, while blue brick was in the worst of taste.

Blue brick came into limited fashion in the early 1960s. Some builders thought the uplifting, bright, regal color would attract tenants. One famous blue-brick postwar building on the corner of Sixty-Fifth and Madison stood in sharp contrast to its stately limestone neighbors. After it converted to co-op, potential buyers would say, "Just don't show me anything in that blue building." It got so hard to sell these apartments that, by 2002, at great expense to the shareholders, the blue brick was jackhammered off and the building was resurfaced with the traditional prewar red. The few others around town followed suit, despite the cost and tenants having to live through a messy three-year project.

For a long time, there were buyers who said, "I don't want anything in a white-brick building." Now there is a new appreciation for white— it matches the current cool design mindset called *midcentury modern.* In New York there is a white-brick building, one of the very first, that has been awarded landmark status despite its plebian beginnings. The Manhattan House, built in 1951 on East Sixty-Sixth Street by the New York Life Insurance Company, spans an entire city block and has the second-largest private garden in the city. The building codes back then allowed for insurance companies to invest in limited-revenue rentals only, not luxury complexes. For example, air-conditioning was considered a luxury and not permitted. However, the builder put in extra electricity to accommodate window air conditioners. The building had wonderful design features that circumvented the building restrictions, and it still had spacious layouts, with many units having three exposures and balconies. It became known as "vanguard-ish" and attracted eminent architects, designers, ad execs, prominent journalists, musicians, and assorted culturati. It is the most successfully designed, midcentury, breezy white-brick building in Manhattan.

Then, starting in the 1990s, the newest buildings began to be called *new development.* Even today, our soaring towers, built for extreme prosperity, are referred to as new development, though they bear little resemblance to the early models, which were designed for regular people. The facades of these usually come in two versions: very modern gleaming glass or, with a nod to prewar, stunning, creamy, soaring sheets of stone.

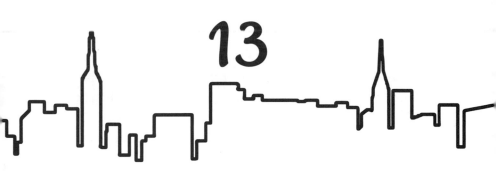

13

The Rennas Hunt for Houses

At the time Donna was searching for her perfect beach abode, Alfred and I were also spending every weekend trolling the streets of Southampton for new FOR SALE signs. The goal was to purchase a vacation home to use as a summer rental, and we had a deadline because the purchase was to be a 1031 tax exchange. We were, as owners, in contract to sell another investment condo and had a time limit on rolling that money into a like-kind property to divert the capital gains taxes on our profit to sometime in the future. *Like-kind property* means that you are selling one investment asset for another similar asset. In the case of real estate, it cannot be your primary residence but can be any kind of real estate in the United States. If you don't roll your capital into another property that is equal to or more expensive than the one you have just sold, then you must the pay tax on your accrued profit. Here's a simple example. You own a house purchased for $50,000 and rent it for two years. You sell it for $100,000. With a $50,000 profit, your tax would normally be based on your income. If you are in a 25-percent tax bracket, that would be $12,500. But because you held on to the property for more than a year, you're entitled to use capital gains tax calculations of 15 percent (plus a minimal amount of local taxes). If you keep the profit, your tax would then be a bit more than $7,500.

You put off paying any tax if you roll all the money into another investment property. You are also making use of the money you would have paid to taxes. Here's an example doing several tax exchanges starting with the first house. You took your initial investment of $50,000, plus your profit of $50,000, and added another $50,000 to invest $150,000 in a bigger house. You rent it for three years, then sell for $300,000. Now your profit is $150,000, but you decide to take that with the rest of what you invested and add another $200,000 to purchase commercial property for $500,000. You rent that for five years. When the lease is up, a fast-food chain approaches you to purchase the property for $1 million.

Now you decide to cash out. To calculate the capital gains tax, your profit basis starts on the first house you bought for $50,000, which means you've made $950,000 gross profit. Then you subtract all of your costs for capital improvements. Let's say you spent a total of $150,000 on capital improvements on all of the properties. Add that to the $50,000. Your base is now $200,000. You add all the closing costs, such as broker fees, maybe another $100,000, bringing your base to $300,000. Your net taxable profit is $1 million minus $300,000—$700,000. It's what you will pay the current federal capital gains tax of 15 percent plus any local capital gains taxes on. Presumably, if you were able to increase your investment money or qualified for a commercial loan, your income also went up along with increased income taxes. Without the benefit of capital gains tax, you might be paying 40 percent income tax, plus your local city and state income taxes, on the $700,000.

We knew that, in Southampton, given the right location, we would be able to carry the costs of a house, taxes, mortgage, etc., through summer rentals. Since we had more than half the purchase price in cash, in the price range we were looking, getting a mortgage was not too difficult. We had chosen to purchase in the village because that meant we would be within two blocks of the train station and near the stop for the luxury commuter bus. A few blocks in the other direction was all the shopping one would need on a summer weekend—highbrow markets with very expensive cheeses and perfect fruit, wonderful clothing shops, art galleries, and the perfect cappuccino, not to mention various kinds restaurants that cater to the locals and summer people, blue-collar, white-collar, and no collar. Finally, no matter the size of one's home, we all got the same resident beach sticker (also known as parking permits), for our cars and were able to park at the most beautiful beaches in the world or a short walk or bicycle ride away.

It was February 2014. Time was running short, and we were dizzy from driving around and around. We looked at every available house within our narrow location and price parameters; then we further narrowed the search to three contenders. Next, Alfred did a financial analysis and determined which house had the best rental potential and long-term upside. This included figuring out the square footage of all three possible houses; the square footage of the land itself, which would dictate how large an expansion we might we be able to build in the future; how much money we would need to put in immediately to obtain the highest possible rent, including whether we'd have to put in central air-conditioning; and whether or not it had a minimum of four bedrooms or the possibility for us to convert another room into a bedroom—ideal to attract the tenant we were seeking—and if there was room to eventually add an in-ground pool. It's really interesting to see how each of these assets added to the rent potential. For instance, if we decided to put in a swimming pool, which in the area would cost a minimum of $70,000, the additional rent over two summer seasons would have paid for the pool.

Satisfied we had done all of our research, which included calling several local brokers we trusted to get potential rental numbers, it was time to call our agent to make an offer. Only problem was she told us she had just learned there was a contract out, even though it had gone on and off the market for two years. What we had learned was that the seller was a rather eccentric woman. No one knew what she did, except tend her garden and ride around in her Porsche, and that every time she had a buyer who signed a contract, she'd change her mind and taken the house off the market. She was the classic seller who was not in a rush. What she hadn't accounted for were two very important things: the market was getting hotter but she wasn't changing her asking price accordingly, and the brokers stopped wasting their time showing it. As Alfred likes to say when we recount this story, "That house was a sleeper."

We were confident the house was already or would soon be worth more than the asking price. The only way for us to secure it and knock the other buyer out of the contract that the seller was sitting on was to go high enough over the asking price to make her feel she'd won the real estate lottery. If we stuck with what she was asking, like many buyers do, we never would have gotten it. So we offered to go $20,000 over ask, which was not really a lot of money in the grand picture. The owner agreed and Cousin Michael was on standby to review the contract as soon as it was sent by the seller's attorney. When the contract was sent out, we were in the city but had requested a clause be added that scanned signatures would be binding. Since Alfred was at Elliman and I was still at Corcoran, he signed and scanned it to me, I signed and scanned it back to Michael, and at the same time, we each contacted our bankers to wire down payment to Michael as well. Michael didn't waste a moment and forwarded the scanned contract to the seller's attorney. The seller must have been sitting right by her attorney's desk, because the countersigned contract was back to us in about three minutes. We were ecstatic! It was a win for both sides. The seller finally got what she felt she was due all along, and we got what we felt was the best deal in the village. Of course, it needed our touch, and with a minimal upgrade by Paul's talented team, we've already been offered $400,000 over what we paid. We are now into our third summer with multiple requests from prospective tenants that start long before the Memorial Day kickoff weekend.

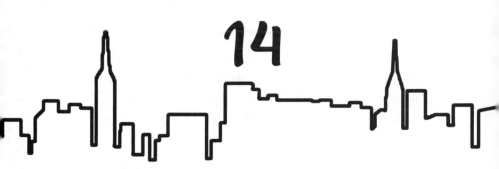

14

Condos, Co-Ops, Condops, and Cockapoos

When it comes to apartments, there are various modes of ownership in Manhattan. A condominium, also referred to as a *condo*, means when one purchases an apartment, they own it to the walls. Just like purchasing a house, there is a deed. The condo owner will also own a percentage of what we call *common spaces*. Common spaces include public hallways, the lobby, the gym, and laundry facilities. The amount of common space owned is calculated based on the size of the apartment, and sponsors who sell the apartments of new-development buildings might include some of this common space in the quoted square footage of the apartment.

When financing to purchase a condominium, one gets a regular mortgage. The condominium board allows for the maximum a bank will lend to the potential purchaser, and the condominium must be on their list of approved buildings. The bank will have a lien on the apartment just like a house. Almost all of the new-development buildings have been built to be condominium ownership. Each condo owner pays a monthly fee for running the building, such as doormen salaries, called *common charges*. Each owner pays their own real estate taxes.

We asked Jonathan J. Miller, president and CEO of Miller Samuel Inc., Real Estate Appraisers & Consultants, to give us a break down of co-op versus condo ownership in Manhattan: "Manhattan is a rental market, despite public perception. About 75 percent of the market is rental and 25 percent is owned. Of that 25 percent, about 75 percent are co-ops and 25 percent are condos. However when I first started appraising in the mid-1980s, co-ops were 85 percent and condos were 15 percent of that 25 percent."

Next, we have the anomaly that is the *condop*, which is not even a real word. This is a wannabe condo living on borrowed land or air— air being very valuable in New York City—and otherwise known as a *land lease*. They are kind of like cockapoos—you're not quite sure what you've got. Sometimes these mixed breeds don't show up on property searches and hardly anyone says, "I want a condop." If you ask ten brokers to define a condop, you will get ten different answers. No one really knows what a condop is. These do have their advantages. They are less costly than condos and easier to get into than a co-op. For savvy buyers who don't want to go the route of buying into a co-op or don't want to spend the extra money it costs to buy the same size home in a condo, a condop, still a well-kept secret, is the way to go, especially when, at this writing, we have few condos priced at over $16,000 per square foot!

Another multi-abode variety worth mentioning is the loft. Loft living started in Soho, which, in the 1950s, had become known as *Hell's Hundred Acres*. It was an industrial area full of sweatshops and small factories, bustling in the daytime but empty and dark at night. It would not be until the 1960s, when artists began to be interested in the high ceilings and many windows of the increasingly empty manufacturing lofts, that the character of the neighborhood began to change. The artists started illegally sleeping in their studios and gradually added showers to the factory bathrooms, as well as rudimentary kitchens. The lofts were usually one big rough space the artists painted all white, with open ceilings revealing all the plumbing and heating ducts, though heat would be turned off after 6:00 PM and all weekend, times that presumably there was no one working.

Many of the original lofts were in buildings with beautiful cast-iron facades. They had huge windows and great character in the hardwood floors meant for factories. Eventually, these buildings were converted to live/work spaces for artists and became legally designated by the city as artist-in-residence (AIR) buildings. The artists were able to purchase their lofts, usually as co-ops. They were cheap back in the '70s, but you had to prove you were really an artist to buy these spaces. This was how Soho and Tribeca got their start as cool neighborhoods to live in. They got to be so cool that, by the '80s, investment bankers wanted to live in lofts too and would get around the AIR designation with some fancy maneuvering, like saying they were a dancer, or their wives or husbands were jewelry designers or the like. They came in and would spend hundreds of thousands to renovate. Hundreds of thousands grew to millions, and before you knew it, by the '90s, most artists could no longer afford to live and work in lofts in downtown Manhattan and had to find new frontiers, such as Bushwick, in Brooklyn.

Then the developers came in and started to build new loft buildings, adding bedrooms and other designated spaces, essentially turning the loft concept right back into traditional apartments with one exception: the open kitchen. Here in New York, everyone used to refer to an open kitchen as a *California kitchen*. No one ever knew why. Even the Californians asked, "What's a California kitchen?"

Now, what was called an *open kitchen* with a mandatory island the size of a small car is simply *the kitchen*.

In the '90s, when traditional lofts were entirely open spaces except for the bathrooms, and this was considered the coolest way to live Downtown, some living Uptown wanted the loft experience without having to move and converted their traditional prewar apartments into lofts by removing the wall between the kitchen and the formal dining room. The fantastic open spaces and kitchens Downtown were the kiss of death to Uptown. No broker, no matter how good, could sell a traditional prewar turned loft. Many advised buyers of prewar apartments never to open the kitchen to the dining room, knowing that when their buyer was ready to trade up, it would be difficult to unload. This has now changed again, and it is imperative that walls can be removed, as buyers now ask, "Can all the walls be taken down?"

We had a high-powered corporate attorney purchasing in a prestigious postwar in the midtown area of Sutton Place. She signed the contract, submitted a completed board application and interview, and was approved by the admissions committee. She pursued the apartment with the assumption that she could take down an offending wall that enclosed, and thereby segregated, the kitchen. After she was told that the wall could not come down due to structural interference, she submitted that she should have been automatically advised of such limitations under the presumption that all preexisting enclosing kitchen walls must come down. On this basis, her attorney demanded that the seller return the down payment and allow her out of the contract. The buyer wasted no time and purchased another apartment where a proper open layout could be achieved, leaving the details of her prior deal to her attorney to sort out.

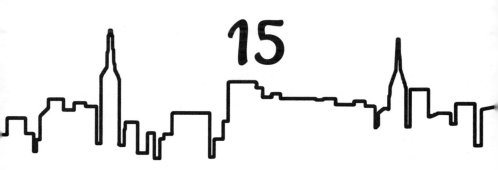

15

Building Tree Forts

Our first childhood summer in our new summer house, we were kept busy with all sorts of home and garden projects. The very first thing we did was go to the local garden center to find trees. We planted two apple trees, two pear trees, a stand of white birch out front, and one skinny, little Japanese maple in the side yard. It was a good start. Then our father put in a vegetable garden. Not all of us were interested in donning boots and raking manure into the sandy soil, but I loved it. I loved being outside, working with my father till we could smell dinner coming from the kitchen. When Dad was back in the city during the week, I would check every day for the first seedlings to pop out of the soil. Then our father put in a circular walkway our mother designed, working under the hot sun till every brick that he used for the edges was set perfectly. Every day that we went to the beach that summer, we'd comb the shore looking for the most perfect, smooth white stones to fill our pails, and then spill them out onto the new path. When it was really hot, we'd forgo hunting for stones, and instead spend hours swimming in the bay while our mother sat under her umbrella. When our father showed up on the weekends, we'd all head to the ocean, where we learned to be fearless diving through the biggest waves, or he would take us fishing, clamming, or snorkeling for conch shells.

By the second summer, and with more homes going up, we were all fascinated with building and designing. There were now a few other families in the neighborhood, living in various versions of our house. One of the mothers who gathered at the beach encouraged our mother to send us over after dinner one evening, so Rosemary and I could play with her daughter and Alfred could play with their son. Donna, who was still too young, stayed home. We were escorted to the daughter's bedroom to view her doll collection, which Rosemary and I found painfully boring, while Alfred got to do "boy stuff" outside with the son. I could hear them running and yelling and having fun, while I endured one of the most boring hours of my life, which I spent formulating an idea to build a tree fort. I couldn't wait to get away with my siblings.

We didn't even wait for our mother to come back and pick us up and instead took off just as the sun went down. I'd had enough of "girl" play, and as we walked home in the dark, Rosemary, Alfred, and I discussed our plans for our first tree fort. We were determined to begin our drawings the next day. As soon as our father arrived, Rosemary and I laid out our plan. To his credit, he looked at our drawing with great seriousness, never once suggesting that dolls or sewing might be more suitable. Then just before dinner, he took all four of us for a walk in the woods to find the most suitable spot and assured us that, if we needed to, cutting certain types of small trees and saplings would actually be good for the larger hardwood trees.

Then we went down to the basement, so he could demonstrate how to use his bow saw and various other tools. We would be allowed to use them, provided we took care of them.

For the next two weeks, we set to work. Rosemary and I spent hours every day cutting down dozens of saplings, even forgoing the beach. It was really hard work, and the bow saw, which had one rounded end and one narrow end, was awkward to use with each of us taking an end like we had seen loggers do on television. We'd have to switch it around when our hands got too sore. Then we had to cut all the smaller, springy branches off. Alfred would help lift and drag, since he was very strong from a young age, and Donna was our tiny helper. Rosemary had the greater tree-climbing abilities, and she'd shimmy up to grab the larger trunks Alfred and I maneuvered up to her, to secure as crossbeams stretched across the stand of trees where each had a crotch about six feet high.

We used medium saplings for our floor, and then built up the sides, alternating the smallest saplings, overlapping each like a log cabin. Then we built a ladder between two trees, with a log bridge to connect to the fort. To discourage our pretend enemies, we sharpened stakes and drove them into the ground all along the bridge. By the second Thursday evening, our father followed us into the woods to inspect our fort. Looking back, I now realize that he was amazed, but he acted very professional, speaking to us like we were a real building crew. When he saw our artfully installed stakes, he calmly suggested we remove them, as we could also be impaled should we lose our balance. Every summer, we had to rebuild after the winter took our fort down, and our construction designs improved. We never used nails, wanting to be as natural as possible. We did make an exception for the use of rope to secure the ladder rungs and create a swing for Donna.

By midsummer, word got around about our cool fort, and all four of us were invited to a fort in the woods built by some of the local boys who lived in the older neighborhood. In those days, you were categorized in one of three ways: locals, who were more like country folk, were year-round residents and did not mix with the summer people; the renters, who no one admired because they often had too many people in one house for the summer; and summer people. We were now summer people, those who owned their houses, only came for the summer season, and had the same parking permit as a local. Not only did the boys have a "no summer kids" rule, but they also had a NO GIRLS ALLOWED sign outside their fort. But even though three of us were summer girls, they were so in awe of what we had built they couldn't help themselves and hoped we would find their in-ground fort as interesting as they found our tree fort. They had dug an impressive hole, kind of like a mini-basement, and used a discarded refrigerator box as a covering. Later on, Rosemary, Alfred, and I discussed how we would have done things differently. I remember thinking how we would have hung some of our artwork, maybe cut a couple of flaps for windows you could peek out of to see unwanted visitors approaching and get some air.

There we were, seven of us squatting in the local boys' fortress. We had climbed down exposed tree roots to get in, which was very cool. It felt a bit like a cave and smelled of earth and cardboard. It was cozy, but I couldn't help but think some saplings suspended for the floor, to shore up the cardboard walls, would have helped things when it rained really hard a few days later and washed most of the boys' hard work away.

Along with our own architectural feat in the woods, new summer houses continued going up in our neighborhood, which we found fascinating to explore. We liked to breathe in the scent of all the freshly sawn wood and stacks of cedar shingles. Sometimes, we helped ourselves to a few scraps of wood for our various projects. We loved our summers.

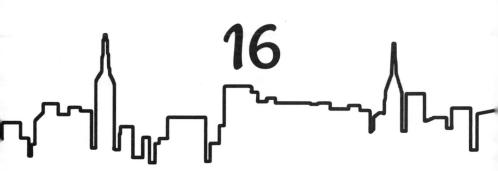

Passing Scrutiny of the Co-Op Board

Purchasing a cooperative apartment is not like any other real estate purchase. The first hurdle is proving to the seller's broker that you have the required cash to purchase and that you are capable of passing the board's scrutiny of financial worthiness, in writing, before your offer is submitted. Each building's board of directors has their own criteria for how much money is acceptable. The last board application Donna, Lenny, and I delivered had ten copies plus the original, and each copy included two three-ring binders, three inches thick, filled till not one more piece of paper could be added. This meant that, piled up, the entire submission of legal forms—financial statement with all bank and investment statements backing up this buyer's liquid net worth, plus real estate, art and antique appraisals, and a slew of reference letters from friends, business associates, bankers, and accountants—was five and a half feet high.

Buyers come out of the co-op board application process feeling like they have passed the bar exam or successfully completed their master's thesis. We agents sit on the edge of our seats along with our buyers and sellers, from contract signing to the email from a building's managing agent with those magical words: "The buyer has been approved." Sometimes there is a *but* or an *if* attached, meaning the buyer is approved under certain conditions. For instance, they may have to put two years of maintenance charges into an escrow account or the board is requesting clarification on the financial statement. Of course, there are the dreaded board turndowns after so much work and time. We can only say to the devastated buyer that it must have been that the board is looking for even stronger financials or the board thought the sale price was too low. This happened to us last year on a very difficult listing, as the living room faced a narrow air shaft to a brick wall. We heard through the super of the building that the president of the board thought the price was too low. We got the buyers to increase their offer by $25,000 and the board turned their decision around and welcomed them to the building.

Board rejections usually occur following review of the applications that are distributed to each of the co-op board members. Rarer are the board rejections that occur after a buyer has been invited to a personal interview. The invitation to an interview implies that the board of directors has already approved the financials and is happy with the buyers' backgrounds, including where they attended school, their employment history, and philanthropic endeavors quietly revealed in the reference letters, and the final step is the in-person assessment. Meetings with the board most often take place in an apartment of one of the members. Though some boards have special common rooms for such occasions or might use the mail room, brokers strongly advise what potential buyers should wear, according to the tenor of the co-op. While a dark suit is almost always appropriate, for certain buildings, it might be suggested a woman wear a conservative, demure dress, minimal jewelry, and no discernable nail polish. Yes, still true in such a liberal city! An interview can last a few minutes or an hour, and some are a casual, more social conversation, looking for common ground, like favorite vacation spots or mutual acquaintances, while others are loaded with tricky questions. Best not to ask anything or act surprised if one of the members throws out a comment about a huge assessment coming up.

We could cite a building or two that pride themselves on more turndowns than approvals, before or after an interview. One building's board of directors has such a reputation for unexplainable and unbelievable turndowns that most brokers won't even show in that building. At the very high end of the scale of cooperative living are those buildings where it is general knowledge that, if you are not a captain of industry or a king or queen with a real crown and *extremely* deep pockets filled with either very old money or very valuable new money, it's not worth calling for information, let alone an appointment. To gain entry for just a preview of an apartment, you need to furnish proof of your worthiness, especially if you are not a recognized VIP or represented by a known and in-the-know broker. There are those who have extreme wealth and fly under the radar, but almost always, they will already know someone who lives in the building or know someone who knows someone.

There are co-ops where board members and their admissions committees simply want a variety of nice neighbors who pay their bills. Others are run as exclusive clubs, where the members want other members to be like they are. From that perspective, why would a bridge club want a member whose every free minute is spent skateboarding, and vice versa? We see some co-op boards turn down potential buyers with no reason given, even if they have the assets and liquidity to close. Since they are privately owned corporations, they do not have to provide a reason. Even when we know that a board is very particular about whom they allow in, there is a line that brokers cannot legally cross, and that is suggesting to a potential buyer that they should not consider a particular building or location. This is called *redlining* for which we could lose our license to sell.

Each version of apartment ownership has its pros and cons. For instance, one may purchase a condominium as an investment property and rent it out without limitation except that each lease be a minimum of one year. In a co-op, a potential tenant must go through nearly the same approval process as a potential buyer, if the board permits rentals. If they do, it is under extenuating circumstances and for a limited time, such as two years out of five. And co-ops have their own ideas about how much a person can finance. The most in Manhattan is 80 percent of the contract price, presuming the appraisal comes in high enough. The average is 65 to 75 percent of the contract price. Then we have buildings in areas such as Park Avenue where the average is less than 50 percent of the contract price. There are buildings that only allow 30-percent or even 0-percent financing. Now just imagine purchasing an eight-room Park Avenue apartment at $8 million. With a permitted 50 percent financing, a buyer must have a $4 million down payment, plus additional liquidity as the co-op may require. The challenge is these buildings do not openly state such requirements. Brokers know from experience that certain buildings will want to see a minimum of three times the purchase price after you close—that means the $4 million down payment, plus $24 million in liquid assets. Liquid means cash, stocks, bonds, and sometimes gold. The value of one's beach house, rare car collection, and even retirement accounts does not count.

A handful of our prewar buildings were built as cooperatives, so people could choose to live among those who might be their friends or associates or go to the same summer communities. Other unwritten conditions, whispered by knowing brokers or alluded to by co-op board presidents or even the doormen, could include what clubs one needs to belong to, how many shareholders you already need to know in the building, and who the beneficiary of your last political fundraiser was.

There are also bylaws and policies one must agree to adhere to if accepted into a co-op. For instance, it must be your primary address; no strollers, shoes, or umbrellas may be left in common halls; 80 percent of the floors must have carpeting; and children may inherit the apartment but do not have a right to move back in unless they pass scrutiny of the board. They also cannot just show up as guests. At certain stylish addresses, one may not have an overnight guest unless the shareholder is in residence. Of course, live-in help is exempt. So if your best buddy wants to use your pad while you're away, just dress him up as the substitute housekeeper. Some buildings require staff to use the service elevator, but hey, so do the celebs like Jay Z and some presidential hopefuls, to avoid their fans and the press. Dog walkers have a free pass to come and go and may even live in the apartment to pet sit while the owners are on vacation. They do not fall under the category of *guest*. Many co-op board applications include an affidavit you must sign and have notarized that states you will not harbor fugitive guests in your apartment when you are not in residence. Further, should you have guests, they must be registered with the concierge and may stay for a limited time only—yes, even if they are your grown children.

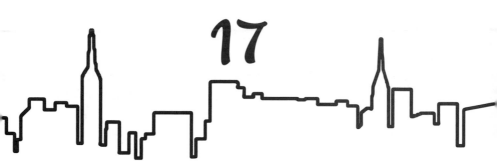

Entitlements and Privileges

A s co-op boards have been slow to change their perspectives on their applications and interview processes, which, as privately owned corporations, they are fully entitled to have, so have our senior socialite brokers been reluctant to change how they do business. This is especially true for those who were the first to forge the agent role in selling co-op apartments back in the 1970s, when Manhattan had mostly rental buildings and a few, very club-like co-op buildings.

"Can you teach a senior social broker who feels entitled to certain privileges to be a business broker?" I asked Alfred.

"If they are young thinking and have motivation and vision, they'll reinvent themselves. And those who have continue their long, successful careers." But there are many who want business to be as they have always known it, putting together sellers and buyers by word of mouth among a privileged few. It was how apartments used to change hands. "Old business practices no longer work. I actually had a white-gloved agent come to me and ask for an advertising budget so she could run some spot ads in the classified section of the newspaper. Can you imagine?" Alfred continued.

"I haven't seen a spot ad in an actual paper since . . . when?" I responded.

"The eighties! This agent is a perfect example. She's been in the business for probably forty years. In the last five she's come into the office twice, and each time there have been greater technological advances that she's missed." Alfred was getting frustrated just telling me about this agent. To his credit, and Douglas Elliman's, these ladies—no gentlemen left in this group—are honored for their long years of service and have been allowed to keep their desks. In this case, the broker also had a sense of advertising entitlement that no longer existed.

"He told her, 'With all due respect, we have not run printed newspaper ads in years. Have you heard of the internet?'" Alfred explained to me. "I said, 'We spend millions of dollars on it annually and you should familiarize yourself with how we now market properties.'" Alfred went on to relate another story of two senior brokers who teamed up to share their business and boost their numbers. Last year they earned $20,000 combined, and they each have the desks they were assigned when they joined the firm.

"They used to be at the top. But we still honor their achievements and knowledge, but mostly, they just like to come to the office," he said with a heavy sigh.

"They want the excursion. It's one of the benefits of brokerage. There's no retirement, and one could look forward to nice long chats in the hallways and ladies' room." I told him. I was thinking about the times I sometimes go a different route to avoid such encounters when I'm in a rush.

"The younger women come to the office in flats or running shoes, then switch to heels. The older women show up in heels, then switch to flats."

"Alfred, all women are entitled to forgo heals at the office, in fact, when running around showing apartments, it's more efficient not to wear heals, especially high ones."

"And back to my ladies, they have built up a history of entitlements and are still ego driven, which is what I love about them, regardless of if they make money or not. Eventually, they all get a great Park Avenue estate sale."

These brokers always live in good buildings, belong to good clubs, wear good silk scarves and kid gloves, and for them, having a good desk as a real estate veteran is also an entitlement.

"I went to buy a new scarf," I started to say, thinking about how one presents oneself is how one is treated, "and you know, Alfred, when you know your entitlements, it shows, and people know it. Take the salespeople at Bergdorf's behind the Hermés scarf counter, for instance. They won't even look at you if don't wear your entitlement, which could include carrying a costly designer purse."

"Then there are the entitlements of customers and sellers. Of course, New Yorkers already feel and behave entitled just by living here."

"We do." I agreed with Alfred regarding New Yorkers feeling entitled. "Just by the fact that we survive so much competition and stress!" I went on to tell him about a rash of buyers with a sense of entitlement. "Some buyers can be abrasive and still truly believe they are being charming. The ones from New York are very upfront in their demands. I like that. Then there are those who want what they want and like to think they can always pull a few strings. They go behind your back."

Fortunately, it's rare, but I've had a few over the years. I had a woman who thought of herself as being the toast of the town from

Hollywood. Not only that, but when she realized she banked at the West Coast outpost of the very same bank that was the executor of the estate that included the sale of the real estate, she felt entitled to purchase the apartment because of the connection—and at a reduced price. Of course, as the bank's broker, I had the fiduciary responsibility to get the highest and best price with the most qualified buyer. My encounter with this entitled woman was astonishing. She called the New York bank, asking for her banker's counterpart, who in turn passed her along to the estate trustee and insisted that I had not submitted her offer. It was not the first time this had happened. She was politely informed that, yes, her offer had been submitted as well as all correspondence she had sent to me, and that no, she was not entitled to pay less than anyone else bidding just because she kept money at the bank, as protecting all of the clients was paramount to the trust they'd built up over many generations.

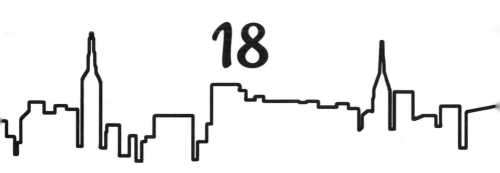

18

Endings and Closings

By mid-March 2014, a little over a year had passed since our mother, Millie, passed away. Our father quietly grieved. They had been so in love. Toward the end, as dementia took its toll, Mom would forget about Dad even if he left the room for just a few minutes. When he'd come back in, she'd hold out her arms as she exclaimed the best she could how happy she was that he'd finally returned, as though he had been gone on a long trip. He'd go to her, and they'd hug and kiss each other, and then she'd glow with contentment. It was really inspiring how he still saw her as the most beautiful woman in the world.

Growing up, we didn't quite realize what a beautiful mother we had. We knew what a good mother and wife she was. She was always enthusiastic about our passions, especially for real estate. I loved to sit at the kitchen table and read the classified ads to her for homes for sale. She'd be preparing dinner and *ooh* at the descriptions. We loved her passion for decorating. No matter how much money our father made, our mother always found ways to make our homes beautiful, often incorporating our help.

When our parents built our modest summer home, it was a luxury, but we believed we were rich. None of our friends in Queens had a house they went to just for the summer, and those long summer days were so glorious. When school ended, our parents would pack up the two cars, our parakeet, our Shetland sheepdog, and the four of us kids, and the summer would stretch out before us. Each summer, our mother came up with different decorating projects. One year we bought an old cocktail table at a local antique store and spent rainy days gluing tiny mosaic tiles all over the top. One of our favorite projects was making paintings on pieces of wood we had found on the scrap piles at building sites. The crews were happy to let us sort through and pick the best pieces. Many of the paintings are still hanging on the walls in that house, which now belongs to our father's sister, who bought it from our parents when money got really tight.

We all have re-created the wonderful luxury of a summer house by the sea. Donna even has the old screen door of her '50s bungalow that bangs closed like the one in our childhood summer home, as everyone goes in and out. And at the end of the day now, we might still be in bathing suits and bare, tanned, sandy feet, kicking back on the deck of one our homes or headed to a favorite dockside bar. I still love how happy and healthy we all look, and how the sea air makes our hair fall in thick, sticky clumps and our lips taste salty. It is a feeling of freedom and flip-flops and remembering youthful kisses behind the dunes, and ice cream and drive-in movies, baked clams you dug up, scaling the fish you caught, and finding your summer friends again and again.

We were all excited when Donna closed on her summer house in 2014. It was a week before our father passed away. He had gone to see it just after she signed the contract. Alfred and I were closing on our investment house a few days later, and we had suggested to Donna that if she wanted to own a piece of it, we would double her investment. She loved the idea that she would have her name on two deeds, no matter the proportion of her ownership. Then, just days after we closed, our father died.

It was a Friday morning, the day he usually went to his physical therapist. He called Alfred to say how cold he was and asked if Alfred would come out to the house and help him. He had never done that before. At 6:00 AM, Alfred jumped in his car and raced to Little Neck. He found Dad in bed, still holding his iPhone. He was ninety-two, had 20/15 vision, supersonic hearing, a genius IQ, and was relatively healthy—except for his heart, I guess.

By the time we all met up in Little Neck, our father's body had already been moved to the local funeral parlor. It seemed like we were just there when our mother died, so the funeral director was used to our morbid sense of humor. "So, is it okay for the deceased to pay for the expenses with a check?" Alfred said, pulling out our father's checkbook and a pen.

"Well, as long as the deceased wrote the check out yesterday. Heh, heh, heh," was the director's response. So we made arrangements for the director to make the arrangements. Our father would join our mother in Calverton, the cemetery for veterans.

It was late by the time we were done at the funeral parlor. We were drained and stunned. We'd thought he had at least another ten years, longevity being prominent in the Renna clan. Since Rosemary and Rico were still scrambling to get back home from Sicily and another wake was scheduled to take place before our father's, we arranged the wake for Monday, when all four of us would be together, and the funeral would be on Tuesday morning. We decided to go to Southampton to wait. It's funny how when someone close to us passes on it causes us to think about their lives, and we talked over the weekend about how he taught us to use a clamming rake, and dive for conch shells, how to bait a hook, and how to use tools to build all those things our mother wanted to make our house beautiful. It then occurred to us that perhaps Dad had missed those summers at the beach as much as we had when we'd been forced to give them up, though he never said a word about it.

That night when we went to dinner, Alfred pulled out some money he'd found when we were looking through our father's files. "Daddy is treating us to dinner," he said. And that was how we celebrated our father's life: toasting to him and others who had gone before. After our mother died, our father's greatest pleasure had been when we took him out and treated him to dinner every week. This time would be no different except it was his turn to pick up the bill.

We all still miss the texts he'd send us, keeping us in the loop about his activities. I think it was also his way to not only stay connected, but also to let us know he was still alive. One day, when Donna and I were in the middle of a meeting, there were simultaneous pings on each of our phones.

"Hi, all. Having TT & HBGGS. LUV, Dad."

What on earth is TT & HBGGs? we had pondered a moment when another set of pings followed. That time, there was a photo to accompany the mystery text. It was a mug of tea, toast, and two hardboiled eggs sitting on a plate.

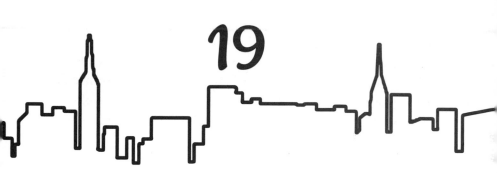

19

Craziest Deals:
Queen of the Board

Co-op boards of directors usually hold a vote for all shareholders to choose their leaders. The positions are the same as other corporations: president, treasurer, secretary. Some buildings are run a bit more like small monarchies, where the president sees themselves more like a king or queen and they reign with their close circle of directors. I once represented a unit ruled by of one of these monarchs.

Before the trustee of an estate could sign the exclusive agreement for me to market the fabulous penthouse apartment that occupied the top two floors of a lovely prewar building, she and I both had to be interviewed by the president of the board. The woman was quite handsome in a regal way; her image could have been on paper money for a small monarchy. She sat on a divan with her long, thin legs carefully crossed to the side, and her hair was pure white and

piled high. She held her head proudly, displaying her most prominent feature, her nose. We sat on small chairs before her, looking
up into her long, narrow nostrils. "I would like to be informed of all
activity, who the potential buyers are, and what they are offering,"
we were duly directed. I was actually quite happy as it meant I had
passed her scrutiny.

The home had not been touched in over fifty years. There was
a gaping hole, large enough for a person to fall through to the floor
below. The walls were crumbling. It was five thousand square feet of
prewar potential with multiple fireplaces and a fabulous terrace—
and would need a couple of million dollars in renovations.

A prominent person in entertainment bid on the apartment,
nickel and diming us for days till we came to an agreement. After con-
ferring with the queen, who said she was not a fan of those in the
music business but she respected him as a self-made man, she gave us
her blessing on the sale. It was very unusual to have what amounted to
preapproval. A contract went out, and three more weeks of negotiating
later, the buyer's attorney finally called me to say his client signed, he
had the contract and deposit in his hands, and would send it out upon
my signing a nondisclosure agreement that no one would ever find
out his client was living in the building. Which was virtually impossible and I had to say no. He then threatened to pull the deal, and my
response was that he should do what's best for his client.

Next, he called the attorney for the estate, who then called me to
say that I should under no circumstances sign such a nondisclosure.
The buyer's broker called begging me to sign. I couldn't blame her; it
was a big deal. Donna and I went for lunch. One bite into my salad, I
got a call from a broker I had known for years. He was in the apartment with his buyers and our assistant, Lenny, who was showing it
as part of our backup plan.

"What do we need to do to get this apartment?" the broker asked.
"Would six million nine hundred do it?"

"No."

"How 'bout seven?"

"No." We kept going till he was a reasonable jump up from the current offer. I called the trustee. "Alison, we've got another offer." As it is her responsibility to push for the highest possible offer, she suggested I go back to the first buyer's broker. Of course the broker was disconcerted, but without theatrics, she promised to get a higher offer. It was the buyer's attorney who called back, now very nervous that his attempting to be a hero for his client may have lost them the apartment. The buyer increased his offer by $1.3 million, no nondisclosure necessary. I called the trustee again.

"Alison, are you sitting down?" I filled her in.

"Oh my, God! I can't believe it. Now what do we do? I don't know. Something just doesn't feel right about this, especially after the hard time the attorney gave us." She and I got the queen on a conference call. The extra money would give the board an even a bigger windfall on their 3 percent flip tax, really a transfer fee, which is based on the sale price. She told us she had googled the original buyer, then watched several episodes of the show he had produced, and that even though she found the violence distasteful, she thought it quite well done. We told her about the higher offer he'd made, way above the asking price. She expressed her astonishment, and we then reviewed the attributes of the two different buyers, presenting each as fairly as possible. While she thought the increased offer was actually in poor taste, she promised to present each buyer with the equal fairness to her board and allow them to decide.

A day later, she called us. The board wanted the second buyer, whose offer was seven figures less than the other one. We were not surprised, as part of their offer letter had included a list of the clubs they belonged to and pointed out that the wife's mother was the president of the Mayflower Society. Certain co-op boards simply cannot resist any connection to those who came over on the Mayflower.

It was a great disappointment to the first buyer, and I was disappointed for him. His attorney accused me of having favored a buyer of my own to get a full commission and of not submitting his client's substantially higher offer, which he was certain no one else had come close to. The estate's attorney assured him that I had, in fact, submitted his client's increased offer, that I was not favoring a direct deal, and that, had he played by the rules, his client would have had the apartment at his original contract price, with the sanction of the president of the board.

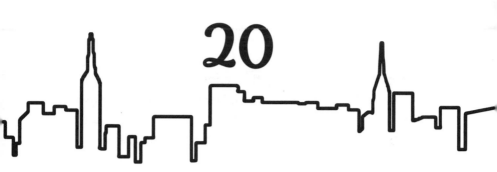

20

Co-Op Board Dog Interviews

W hile we are on the subject of potential co-op board interview-
ees, we mustn't forget the dogs. They too must prove their
worthiness. With buildings that permit pets, cats are given a free
pass on the interview, but not dogs. Some are open to cats and dogs
in limited numbers, like one or two pets at the most, but there are
often weight maximums and breed restrictions for dogs.

"Alfred, can you imagine preparing a dog for the co-op interview?" I asked my brother one day.

"They must be told to be absolutely well-behaved and not bark
at inappropriate moments," he replied.

"It is also vital that the dog gets groomed beforehand, just as any
people going to an interview will look as nice as they can," I said.
"And before show time, have a little chow time, just in case there

are any good cooking smells wafting about at the interview, most of which take place in the evenings. And be sure to take the dog to use the bathroom before entering the building."

"A good dog trainer will be able to show your dog the proper way to behave during introductions," Alfred added. "Not a bad time for that refresher course for both buyer and dog, if needed. They should not sit until invited to do so and, when addressed, lift their paw."

"And please don't drug your dog or yourself into a stupor, no matter how nervous everyone is. It's very obvious and will raise a red flag to the watchdog of the interview committee, which every building has."

Deals with dogs can be very tricky. Folks who come from a house may not even consider that their dog would not be welcome into the building they hope dearly to live in. We confirm the rules whenever we have a new listing. And just because one might see dogs being escorted through the lobby by their dog walkers, this does not mean a new buyer may bring in their dog. It could very well be that the building changed to a no-pets policy, except those already in residence that were grandfathered in.

There are some dog-loving owners who get around new rules by adopting a dog that looks like their recently deceased dog, or even a sick dog that is near passing. In the case of overlap, the younger dog is given the same name, and the dogs are walked at separate times, so as to appear to be the same dog. In another dog-lovers' deal, the buyer claimed she had two miniature wirehaired dachshunds. The building she was purchasing in only allowed one dog per household. Somehow, she got permission to have the two adorable dogs, Lilly and Pulitzer, to live in the building. All three met with and passed the board and moved in. Only thing was, she really had four miniature dachshunds, but easily negotiated this hiccup by walking them only two at a time, and staggering the walk times calling each pair by the same names.

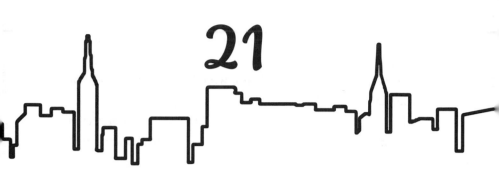

21

Divine Design of the Weekend Warriors!

After the funeral, we all decided to take the rest of the week off and head back to Southampton. It also gave us a chance to spend time with Rosemary and Rico before they headed back to Sicily. While having coffee the next morning, three things occurred to us.

The first was that we no longer had parents. It was now just the four us. We were blessed that we had our mother and father for so much of our adult lives. It made us feel younger than we were. Our parents' maxim was to deny aging, and I can assure you, we are often immature enough to show we are living that idea.

The second thing that occurred to us was that we had just inherited a house and fifty years of possessions. In addition to all of the family treasures and our parents' personal belongings that we would need to sort through, we also inherited the bursting file cabinets and shelves in our father's office, which took up the entire basement, den, and part of the garage. There were boxes that he had not even opened in decades.

Third, somewhere in the midst of our thoughts concerning the task before us, we all came to realize that within ten days, our baby sister, Donna, had gone from no real estate portfolio to owning at least a piece of three houses.

Alfred and I decided to head off to a yoga class and try to clear our thoughts. We now had two houses to take care of, one that needed to be emptied out and one that needed to be filled up. That was not even taking into account the fact the Alfred was working on plans to renovate and expand his own home, and Paul and I were building our Southampton house.

After yoga, we headed to the Village Cheese Shop on Main Street for breakfast and lattes. No sooner did we order our egg and crispy bacon on everything flagels (flat bagels), when in came Sherry. Sherry, an agent with the Douglas Elliman Southampton office, was the broker Donna had used to find her house. Every move she makes is quick; even her hair is clipped into a pixie cut that barely needs the swipe of a comb and makes her big, beautiful, brown eyes appear even larger. "Oh hi, I'm so busy. How are you guys? Listen to this: Alfred, I just sold a house right here in your neighborhood in one minute. It's on Burnett, right here," she happily exclaimed and pointed over her shoulder.

"Oh, I bet it's the brand-new shingled spec house. I've been following the construction all winter. Can we see it?" Alfred replied.

"That's the one, and absolutely, I can show it to you right now." Coffees and flagels in hand, we jumped into the car and sped all of one block to the jaw-dropping, beautiful home. We couldn't help commenting on the gorgeous furniture, and Sherry announced, "Everything is available for sale!"

Our eyebrows went up. We needed everything for the house we'd bought to rent. With hearts racing, our design vision went from being very budget conscious to tripling in cost. That first day, we carefully chose a few basic items that included a king-sized bed. It was a perfect beach house choice, a creamy-white headboard that had a lovely, open bamboo design. The three of us were standing in the master bedroom when Sherry called her client, her former sister-in-law Gina, to tell her our offer. We could hear Gina's barking laugh, then scream, "It's too low! Okay I'll take it." We figured she was taking a low offer because she had to quickly empty the house for the new owners.

Sherry had to pull the phone away from her ear. We yelled back our thanks and did a little more wandering and considering. Meanwhile, Paul called a couple of his guys to come and pick up the bed. The open design of the headboard enabled us to position it in front of a window. We knew that once we had flowing, semi-sheer drapes behind it, the southern light would still stream in.

After that decorating find, we headed to some of the local design shops. At an English furniture store, we saw the perfect end tables for the living room. They had a great roughness to them yet a beautiful, intricate base that reminded me of the Eiffel Tower. With the typical Hamptons high prices and low designer discount, they were $1,350 each. We took photos and left the tables behind, but I couldn't get them out of my mind. At another store, we found the perfect lamps for those tables—over scaled clear glass with polished nickel bases that glittered, and linen barrel shades. They were the perfect contrast to those expensive tables; plus, we needed to really boost the lack of architectural design of the living room, which was basically a white box.

Late in the afternoon, we were back at Alfred's house. He pulled up a photo he had taken of a tag that hung under the dining table back at Gina's spec house. He went on the website Noirfurniturela .com and scrolled for a few minutes, and there were those beauties.

The site was for designers and retailers, so you had to fill out an application; then they assigned a rep to you who would send spread-sheets of the discounted prices. The discounts increased the higher the quantity ordered. We bought those same tables for $481 apiece, along with hammered-nickel bedside tables and a distressed white dresser for the master bedroom. The site also had a lighting depart-ment, and we found perfect glass lamps the color of sea glass for one of the guest bedrooms. We were on a roll and feeling like those designers on TV who fix up a whole house on a weekend.

The next day, we called Sandy to ask if the thick-glass coffee table with four-inch, thick round Plexiglas legs with a touch of brass detail was still available. We ran over to take another look. This time Gina was there in person, a sexy, blue-eyed, bigger-than-life blond, clunking around in clogs, with a booming voice that could fill a con-struction site and have crews racing to fulfill her commands. That is Gina, and that is what she does—builds, designs, sells. We were so inspired by her energy, talent, and laugh; we all hit it off immediately. "Gina, what do you want for that old table?" Alfred asked.

"Five hundred dollars and not a dime less!" she said.

Alfred shot back, "Four hundred dollars. Not a penny more."

"Done! But I want cash dollars."

"Deal!" You'd have thought these two were cousins.

Paul sent his building crew for another pick up. While we were there, we took a second look at the dining chairs. We were already envisioning a Saarinen-like table for the kitchen, which we found online for under $1,000 and realized Gina's chairs would go with it perfectly, so we accepted her lowest offer and had the crew pick those up as well. They had linen slipcovers that could be easily washed and arms that made them really comfortable. Pottery Barn was our next stop for the typical big, soft sofa and chair that have white denim very durable and washable slipcovers and are in almost every home in the Hamptons. Then the West Elm website for more bed frames and side tables, and we signed up for their designer trade program to buy them at discount.

Sisal and various other natural rugs are perfect for a beach house primarily because they feel great in hot weather and are inexpensive. We went to our favorite sisal rug man, who gives us great discounts because we send everyone we know to him. Last, we perused the storage room in Alfred's basement, where we both had stuff sitting for years, and we found all the rest to fill in: tables, lamps, and wonderful paintings.

It was exhilarating and very satisfying to see our house come together in six weeks. Like many siblings, we love to reminisce about favorite memories, especially serendipitous ones, funny conversations, and adrenaline-inducing design moments. We also love remembering our parents and talking about things they might have said or thought. When we sat back and admired our decorating at the house we now call North Main, we thought about how our father would have approved of the fine job we did renting it right away and how our mother would have loved decorating it with us.

"And let's not forget," I reminded Alfred, "that we started off with four light fixtures from Home Depot figuring we'd go cheap but in good taste." And I might add, they do look good.

"The better furnishings got us more money," Alfred added with a satisfied glow. We ended up being the nicest rental available in the category. All we did rang true to what I call the magic of momentum. We kept pressing forward, from the house search, to the analysis, to the orchid that perfectly picked up the colors of the paintings of swimmers hanging in the living room—another design touch we borrowed from Gina. Soon the brokers arrived for our open house, where even the Bellinis matched the artwork. It seemed everything we needed just fell into place, and the first prospective tenant who walked in the door took it for the full summer season.

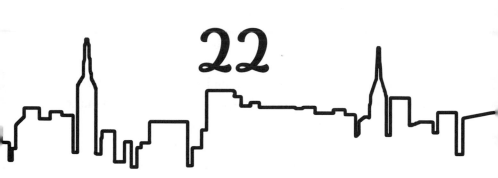

22

Rental Buildings:
High and Low

The newest rental buildings are built much like the newest condos—as high as the developers can get a building permit for. Sometimes, they have been able to go higher than zoning permitted if they included lower-income housing. In order to entice high-end purchasers to buy and high-end renters to rent in the same building as those who were considerably less financially fortunate, the developers came up with a strategy to make it feel like different buildings. There would be two separate entrances and two separate lobbies— one off on the side street, kind of like where the service entrance might be a few feet away, and the main entry and lobby on the avenue or more desirable location for the more glamorous approach to the building, along with a substantial lobby that included not only doormen, but also a concierge. Of course there were those civil

rights–minded people that were up in arms over the disparity, calling it *the poor door*, so a lot of the developers said forget it.

There are still rent-controlled and rent-stabilized leases, which
protect tenants' rights by controlling the amount a landlord can charge.
Most of these tend to be in low-rise, prewar, and older post war buildings. You cannot look for one of these elusive properties. They find you,
and once you have one, you never ever give it up. You design your life
to protect your lease, and with all the extra money, you buy a house in
Rhinebeck. There have been generations of family disputes; there have
been murders and marriages all based on the coveted rent-stabilized
lease. One thing we can say: it has been the foundation for many life-
long marriages that would have otherwise broken up. We have an
acquaintance that married a gay flight attendant for flight benefits and
moved into his apartment as his roommate. He happened to live in
an incredible prewar three-bedroom penthouse with a south-facing
wraparound terrace and open skyline views. Gertie played the happy
housewife, flying all around the world at every chance she got: weekends in Paris, shopping trips to Rome, a spa in Hungary that she said
made her feel like Penelope Cruz.

Then one day, her husband fell ill and soon passed away. Since
his fantastic penthouse was rent stabilized, Gertie was entitled to
stay, possibly forever if her income didn't go up too high and exceed
the maximum income allowed to maintain such low rent leases. So
then, we all understood how she, a lifer waitress at a historic eatery,
was able to afford such a luxurious lifestyle. There are sixty-year-olds
who have moved in with their mothers, perhaps not removing the
life support till they could prove their two years in residence. There
have been scams with grandparents and illegal sublets and all sorts
of check finagling and offshore accounts for income diversion to
maintain the lower income required once the rent reaches a certain
threshold. These tenants will go so far as to do jury duty just to prove
their residency.

23

Under the Sicilian Moon

"**C**iao, Romeo!" Rosemary and I were on FaceTime, and she was reading a novella-length text to me that she had sent to a guy she had met at her Italian language class here in the states. She had now been spending more time in Sicily with her nightmare renovations on her palazzo overlooking the Mediterranean Sea. "*Come stai?* Hope all is well with you."

"Rose," I interrupted, "I've got to get to the office. Could you get to the heart of it?"

"Okay, okay. So, where was I?" She went on to read her saga that in moments seemed to go down to all levels of anguish and back up again to awe and euphoria. Every Sicilian from the real estate broker and the architect, to the multitudes of contractors and the bureaucratic, rubber-stamping clerks had made life a living hell, taking advantage of her at every turn during the nearly impossible renovations.

"Rosemary, Sicily has its own laws," I reminded her. "The mafia has the run of it, and everyone plays by those rules. What did you expect?" The rest of us were concerned that she was pouring money into the project beyond what the properties were worth. But she was in so deep, it was impossible to stop.

Undaunted as she was on her crazy project, she was as intent on reading the entire message to me. "Every morning I wake up to the sun rising over the sea and the sound of the waves," she went on. We had all been there for Thanksgiving the year before and had ended up staying right through New Year's Eve. We saw the sun setting and the moon rising on the water. I decided I might as well get ready for work as she read and put her on speaker.

"Every morning I hear two scooters, driven by two fishermen. They like to park right outside my door, rev their engines as they back up into place, all the while shouting over the whine of the little motors. The diesel exhaust wafts into the house and burns my nostrils. I listen, trying to interpret their language, which sounds kind of like Italian but not. It takes them twenty minutes to pull on their scuba gear and smoke several cigarettes, also burning my nostrils. Just as I'm about to shout out the window and tell them to shut up and put out their cigarettes, they're headed down the stairs of the seawall to the beach, their voices fading, then silence as they slip under the water looking for octopus and sea urchin or, what they say here in Sicily, *polipo* and *ricci*."

Every day, Rosemary wrestles with multiple problems that wrap themselves around her and her bank account like an octopus. She had to get official authorization to restart the work that had been illegally started without her knowledge. Her first architect had submitted plans that were rejected, but he and his contractors kept it a secret in order to continue milking her for money. She finally found out because one day, with the idea that she should check with the building department to confirm that everything was in order, she found one of the officials had a foot-high file on her, sitting right there on his desk. There was no authorization for the work. The following months were spent with Rosemary jumping through dozens of hoops and paying through the nose for more certifications, declarations, authorizations, and anything the locals could come up with. For every piece of paper, they would send her to the *tabaccheria* to buy *francobolli*, tax stamps, to show she had paid a fee to the state, or the mafia, for a stamp on her paperwork, and before they would stamp it with the official stamp. The stamps were required for every piece of documentation she needed, and she needed many. She was now paying an engineer thousands of euros more for proper measurements, calculations, formulations, and permeations. She would get the tax stamps in order, so she could get final approval. Then just as she thought it was all in order, another local official would decide she must conduct an energy plan that showed how much heat or air-conditioning escapes from the apartments. The irony being, she was not permitted to use the brand-new heat and AC units mounted on the rear of the building, out of public view, as they were illegal—illegal despite the fact that hundreds are mounted in plain view on virtually every building on the island of Ortigia.

Getting around this hurdle would necessitate several more visits—to the commune officials, then to the *tabaccheria*, and back to the official offices. Clearly the official had a cousin in the energy escaping business. It was yet another shakedown. Rosemary's engineer in true Sicilian style, had the photos of the building photo shopped, eliminating the offending units.

On New Year's Eve, when we were all there, it had snowed—very rare for the Mediterranean Island. The next night, there was an incredible storm with high winds that blew debris into the apartment upstairs, through the doors that were yet to be sealed by the *bastardo* door-installing subcontractor. When my brother woke up, he was covered with North African sand and the building's crumbling stucco. A sea of rainwater flooded through the supposedly sealed ground-floor apartment doors.

By day three, we had all noticed mold was growing on all the newly plastered walls, and the heavy moisture also caused the fresh paint to peel all over the place, making it look like a forest of shagbark hickory trees. Then, with all the extra showers, loads of laundry, and two dozen rolls of toilet paper, the family left for New York, and Rosemary was left with a clogged septic system that backed up into the twenty-one-foot deep antique well that she'd dumped thousands of euros into, to preserve for mankind.

Now she had to find someone to pump out the water. To add insult to injury, one of the nasty neighbors had been putting piles of dog doo into her big beautiful cement pots that she'd paid a boatload to ship from Southampton, and that ironically were made in Italy. Then she paid another boatload to yet another architect to submit plans for authorization to place the aforementioned pots in front of the house.

I continued to race around getting dressed as she read, not missing too many details.

"Notwithstanding being a victim of organized questionable activity to elicit money from me, I also had two dead pigeons at my back door, scissors stuck in my side door, my car keyed, and a letter from an attorney representing the first architect trying to extort 15,000 euros from me for services he had not rendered. It was getting harder to see the beauty of the place when I have had to wade through a sea of *merda*."

It seemed to me that after generations of living in Ortigia, even a family that emigrated from neighboring Catania, were still considered aliens. Despite being an American woman, and single, and knowing she would never be embraced there, she had forged ahead, determined to complete the work.

"Then I watched the sun setting and the sky turning an incredible purple," she continued to read her story. "A rainbow came down from heaven and plunged into the sea. It made me think that perhaps I shouldn't be so hasty. Instead, I'll rent the apartments out, get some income, and give the place more time before deciding to sell. Settled with this plan, I went to use one of the upstairs bathrooms, and suddenly, the toilet tilted to its side, nearly throwing me to the beautiful ceramic tile floor. *Merda!* I thought, as I leaped off. The last plumber had asked me if he could borrow my American measuring tape, giving me pause as to what he needed to measure in inches. The bastardo had apparently shoved the tape measure under the wall-mounted designer toilet to steady it."

She finally ended her text with a "big hug" to her classmate. *Abbraccione.*

24

The Locals and How to Be
a True New Yorker

Unlike other parts of the world where you are considered a local only after several generations of owning and tilling the land, one becomes a full-fledged New Yorker upon successfully completing the New York City triathlon. The competition includes the following:

1) Taking the subway at rush hour, free standing on the train at full speed, while schlepping several shopping bags and emerging from the underground unscathed and able to proclaim it the best transportation ever.

2) Speed walking faster than the bag-laden food delivery persons on wobbling bikes, the Kamikaze taxis drivers, and the lost drivers from Jersey.

3) Completing the shopping obstacle courses which are: finding the hidden salespeople and getting one to find your underwear size

at Bloomingdale's, finding anything larger than a size two at Barneys, and securing a pair of shoes in your size on the first day of the winter sales at Bergdorf's. You may get extra points if you shopped for cheese at Fairway and make it to the checkout without getting rammed by one of the tough old ladies who have their own contest of seeing how many Achilles tendons they can sever with their wagons.

Alternatively, if you can articulate your New York real estate experience in an entertaining way, thereby capturing the complete attention of other New Yorkers, whether it is through a marathon tour of homes with a broker or a negotiating war story, such as signing a lease for an apartment you just viewed in the dark with other potential tenants circling you like hungry sharks or surviving bidding on an apartment, then you may immediately claim your status as a New Yorker.

There is another qualifier. *New Yorker* really means one who resides in Manhattan, even though, technically speaking, Queens, Brooklyn, the Bronx, and Staten Island are in the city limits. In order to commute on and off the island of Manhattan, which is central to the boroughs, you must cross the rivers that surround it via a bridge, tunnel, ferry, or helicopter. This means gaining access to Manhattan is the same from all other boroughs—mostly bridge and tunnel. The term *bridge-and-tunnel crowd*, coined back in the disco days of the 1970s and '80s, refers to those not residing on the island of Manhattan, because they took either a bridge or a tunnel to reach the clubs of Manhattan.

These folks commuted in on a Saturday night with attitudes all their own. B&T people love a show, shopping, dining, and, for the younger late-night crowd, clubbing. There have been some very interesting developments concerning the boroughs recently. Brooklyn is hot—so hot, it is cooler to say you live in Brooklyn than Manhattan, though it is not cool to say you were born there. Of course, in a few short years, it will be.

Not all of Brooklyn is cool. Those cool areas are currently at about 20 percent of the vast borough, but the part that is included is the area we like to call "Manhattlyn," a portmanteau (a combination of words), which Alfred and I believe will catch on. The neighborhoods that make up Manhattlyn are downtown Manhattan—that includes Soho, Tribeca, the Lower East Side, and the Financial District— and, in Brooklyn: DUMBO, Brooklyn Heights, Cobble Hill, Carroll Gardens, Red Hook, Park Slope, Prospect Heights, Fort Greene, and Williamsburg. The hipsters can take the party train, also known as the L train, to Bushwick. This subway is often packed with young revelers headed home to the Brooklyn burbs, or young Manhattanites heading to Brooklyn to party. To the unknown, the streets may look foreboding and desolate at night and the buildings abandoned and industrial, but all is not what it seems. Behind those graffitied, steel, corrugated walls are hordes of locals and Manhattanites partying, ogling artwork, and sipping cheap white wine, or negotiating for the next table in the hottest restaurants.

Then there is what we think of as the sixth borough: New Jersey (even though most New Yorkers think that the United States ends on the eastern shore of the Hudson River). We also believe, along with most of our newcomers, that people from New Jersey can't drive. They also can't pump their own gas. Jersey, the Garden State, is one of only two states in all the United States where it is illegal to fill 'er up yourself. Come to your own conclusion about their auto aptitude. New Jersey folks come in over or under the Hudson River and almost always with their big-ass cars. "If they can't be trusted to pump their own gas, why let them cross the state line?" The answer, though we like to make fun of them, is it has always been the tradition of our island to welcome all immigrants, whether you are from across the rivers or across the oceans.

25

Last-Minute Holiday Plans

Four days before Christmas 2015, the office was as quiet as a country church on confessional night. If there is a ring, buzz, or snippet of a cell phone song, it is always family, friends, or boyfriends. This time, it was Rosemary.

"So, Jo, when are we leaving for Southampton? Are we still going tomorrow?" We were all converging on North Main, our little, by Southampton standards, rental for a holiday stay. This year, no one wanted to fly all the way to Sicily again, and Rosemary, who had traveled back to the States in the summer, was happy to stay longer in New York. Paul and I gave up roughing it at our house, where we hadn't yet closed up the walls but which was perfectly lovely for the summer. We moved toothbrushes, Nescafé milk frother, and furry slippers down the road, as did Alfred, who had spent last summer's weekends carrying a laundry basket from his trunk to whoever's house he was crashing in. Our summer tenants were gone, and we had reclaimed our bedrooms till next Memorial Day, when they would return.

"Let's leave Wednesday. I'm not ready for a Tuesday exit." Exiting Manhattan for the Hamptons during the holidays takes careful planning—which day, what time, which route, and whether or not to stop at HomeGoods, a discount store in Riverhead that's chock-full of closeouts from area rugs to nonstick frying pans. It's a treasure hunter's fantasy come true, if you go in for knockoffs and chemical emissions.

"Oh good, me neither. I'm still unpacking from Italy."

"Maybe you shouldn't bother—just live out of your suitcase."

"Yeah, I might as well. Sometimes I don't even know where I am when I wake up."

We made our plan, and I got back to tying up business till the first week of January. In the Renna family, all plans are subject to change. Most plans are made at the spur of the moment. A few Saturdays ago, Alfred, Cousin Michael, and I were out cruising for open houses in Southampton. "Michael," I ventured while it was still relatively early in the afternoon, though it was already feeling like dusk, "what are you doing for dinner tonight? Should we all meet at Little Red?"

"Ah, well, I don't know. It's still too early to make a commitment." Alfred and Michael, while first cousins, might as well be twins. These two grown men are so true to Renna form—they are both still single, not wanting to fall into a committed relationship too early in life. Alfred circumvents his hesitation with a do-it-right-now kind of plan.

"How about we go to Little Red right now for a drink and little late lunch?"

All the Rennas grew up with procrastination and last-minute planning. It's why we all went to Italy for Thanksgiving last year and didn't return till after New Year, extending our stay one week at a time. It drives Paul crazy that we don't plan. He likes a good plan. It took me five years to realize it's because he's a builder and builders need a plan.

Into the third week of our elongated, unplanned Italy stay, he had asked me about why it was so hard to choose a restaurant every lunch and dinner time. "Look, I'm not complaining, but when we're all traveling together. Why does it take two hours to choose a place to eat?"

"Because that's what one does in Italy. You walk around, you look in the window to see what it looks like, and you step inside to get a feel, a scent of what's cooking. You might see what the appetizer table has to offer, what kind of reception we get. Not all restaurants in Italy are fabulous. They used to be, but all those grandmothers in the kitchen cooking generations' old secret family recipes have died off, the kids have emigrated, and many of the restaurants have cooks from Albania and Africa who don't know how to cook pasta to the perfect al dente."

"I see. So, maybe we could start out before we get hungry?"

"We could, but things don't get going in Italy till at least nine in the evening." Since then, Paul has eaten more for lunch, and I tell him, "Okay, the plan is to walk around, maybe do a little shopping, and see if we find a new great place to dine." More often than not, we make a plan; then, one of us changes the plan. If one of us doesn't want to do it, whatever it is, we all change the plan. When we find a good restaurant, if the table is not right, we'll ask to move. If that's not perfect, we'll make adjustments, moving chairs, tables, and decor. It drives a lot of people crazy. It's the same with hotels—we never take the first rooms we're shown, not even the second or third. Alfred has been known to preview five or even six rooms, take a break for lunch, and then continue till he finds the perfect fit. At one of our favorite hotels in Rome, when we walk in, the concierge grabs the keys for every available room.

Staying in New York this year, it was easy to decide at the last moment, that we—Alfred, Rosemary, Paul, and I—would stay for a full two weeks at North Main and act as if we were traveling abroad, but it was actually more like reliving our childhood in Little Neck, with our parents away on vacation. We did whatever we wanted. Mostly, we were all looking to do as much nothing as possible. Each day, as the moment presented itself, we made a short-term plan. We went to Lynch's and found a perfect Christmas tree. Since both Alfred and I had most of our belongings in storage, we needed a tree stand, lights, and a few ornaments. Lynch's will deliver, so the tree came in the front door already in its stand. The delivery guys made a few adjustments, and it was just right. In a few minutes, we had hung what we had to decorate it.

As our lazy days went by, anything we had was added to the tree. Someone had sent a box of cookies, each wrapped in little colorful packages. Donna, who was going back and forth to her house with Michael, hung the cookies on the tree. Any ribbons that came to us on gifts or bottles of wine as friends and cousins stopped by got tied on the tree. Each night, whoever felt like cooking did. When Christmas was only a couple of days away, we decided that we should exchange gifts. We all went to different towns to shop, filled little holiday shopping bags, and had gifts wrapped or used tissue paper for a quick roll around. Lazy? Yes. We all have had our fill of wrapping dozens of presents. Right through till we were grownups, our parents treated the holidays no differently than when we were kids. Christmas meant piles of presents. In the lean years, there were fewer. We never stopped our family tradition, but now we don't want to open presents all morning. We want to make our coffee, admire our tree, open a few little things—mostly kitchen gadgets or something funny—hang around in our pajamas, eat cookies, and then get around to putting a roast in the oven. No one ever knows what time we'll eat.

Each night, we all watched *How to Get Away with Murder*. As soon as we cleaned up after dinner, we'd put on sweatpants or pajamas and curl up in our favorite spots. Alfred and I had put in a sixty-inch high-definition television. I had not watched television in years, and I was hooked to the bingeing craze. One night, we all fell asleep. The show went on. I heard Rosemary snoring, Alfred groaning, and Paul grinding his teeth.

"Hey," I called out, "we all fell asleep."

"What happened?"

"Can we go back? "What'd I miss?" How long was I sleeping?"

One afternoon, we all had the idea that we should go to Hampton Bays for a steak dinner at the Inn Between, then saunter over to the movie theater for a holiday show. Midway through, tired of chewing our tough steaks, Alfred said, "I feel like baking."

Rosemary said, "I'd rather watch our show."

Paul said, "I can't wait to see what happens."

We asked for the bill. The waitress presumed we wanted takeout containers and brought them over. "We don't need those. Thanks anyway," I said. We skipped the movie and headed right over to King Kullen supermarket and filled our baskets with all sorts of baking ingredients and pans. That night, Alfred made a fruit tart. We ate it all while we watched TV. The next night, Rosemary made cookies. By then, we were staying up till 3:00 AM.

On the morning of New Year's Eve, we called around to see if some of our favorite Renna cousins were out. If they were, like us, they probably had not planned a thing yet. We were right: they hadn't planned anything. That night we all had a great time celebrating the New Year. Even Cousin Michael, whom we promised we'd have the game on for, committed to joining us. Of course, we knew he would not have wanted to spend the holiday without us.

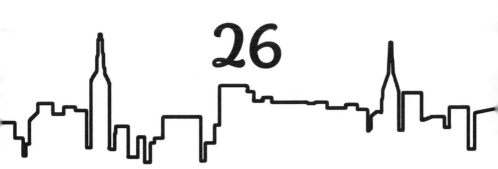

26

The War of Lobby Holiday Decor

It seems each holiday season we all love to relate stories of our other Christmases, how many presents we used to get, when a bicycle or other really special presents were found by the tree, how we loved to spoil our nephew, and how much fun we always had. As a family, we still do, but for different reasons. The presents are less important than enjoying our time together.

Being politically correct with the holidays has infiltrated various aspects of our business, beyond no longer saying "Merry Christmas." Shareholders of various co-ops have started to voice their opinions about decorations that seem unfair. I was telling Alfred about one rather special building over coffee during our holiday stay at North Main. We were sitting in the kitchen.

"We've finally reached that point in New York where not only the menorah should have equal time as the Christmas tree, but it should also be as big," Alfred said.

"That's true, Alfred, and why not? One of the biggest shareholder disagreements recently was over a tree."

"A 'disagreement' as in a brouhaha?"

"Yes, it had everyone up in arms at an established prewar cooperative on the Upper East Side where some of the newer tenants decided that the Christmas tree should not be taller than the menorah."

"Where do you find a menorah as high as Christmas tree?" he asked, chewing another buttery holiday cookie in the shape of an angel.

"Exactly, and no one wanted one of those blow-up lawn menorahs."

"Do they exist?"

"I don't know, but this change of the tree was following fifty-five years of tradition. The original owner of the building who converted—"

"He converted?"

"He converted the building, Alfred."

"Oh . . . that kind of conversion. I thought you were going to say he converted and wanted to switch to a menorah."

"No, he always had both." I went on to tell him about the owner. When the man converted the building from a rental to a co-op, his final request was that the new board would continue the tradition, not just of having a menorah and a tree, but also that the tree had to come from the same family, who has a Christmas tree farm somewhere up in Quebec. The deal he had made a couple of generations before was that they would bring a tall, narrow tree. They took special care pruning multiple trees for years so that each Christmas they had the perfect shape to fit the small lobby, allow tenants to get by to the elevator, and still be twelve feet high. The tree farmers would give a tree to the building, also erecting and decorating it. In return, the owner let them use the doorman facilities down in the basement, where they could get warm, have a meal, and take showers. Most tree sellers travel into Manhattan to set up shop on the sidewalk, and rough it living out of their truck for the season. They rely on nearby businesses to allow them use of a bathroom. Some may not get to take a shower till that last tree is sold.

"I always wondered what those tree guys did," Alfred said, opening the refrigerator looking for leftovers. "They're open twenty-four hours a day till Christmas Eve, starting like a month before."

"I asked once, and one guy told me they took turns sleeping in their truck. But this family was lucky. It was good old-fashioned bartering."

The owner of the building sold the apartments at very affordable prices as well. For those tenants who did not have the money, he secretly took less and transferred the stocks to them anyway. What no one knew till he passed away was that he had no family. "So of course," I continued, "the building continued the menorah and tree tradition. But here it is, years later, and there are new people buying into the building and some feel that there was holiday inequality."

"I know what they mean." Alfred gave up on leftovers and grabbed another cookie. This one had green sprinkles and was in the shape of Christmas tree. "When we were growing up, our Jewish friends were envious of our Christmas trees and all the presents we got, and we were envious because we got presents for only one day and they got presents for eight."

The challenges with ensuring holiday symbol equality are many. To start, for this particular building, the job fell to the building superintendent whose first language was not English and who missed a few nuances. Also, how does one find a large enough menorah? The biggest one I've ever seen is outside of the southwest corner of Central Park, where, in recent years, a two-story menorah is put up each season as an art installation. Where was the super going to find a menorah larger than a regular candelabra? And I'm sure he wondered why all the fuss after all these years. He thought everyone enjoyed a pine-fresh-smelling tree in their lobby, twinkling with lights and wrapped boxes tied up with bows beneath it.

Since many of the board members were heading out of town for the holidays and, well, most of the winter, the super was left to work out the details to keep those who stayed behind happy. That year, when the tree brothers showed up, he asked if they could cut the tree down a bit. They were confused—clearly the tree was already cut down. The super showed them the menorah, made various hand signals, and the brothers nodded with understanding, said they'd get the job done, and went to their truck for the tools and decorations. As they left the lobby, the super was called to an emergency—someone's bathtub was leaking down to the next apartment. When he finally returned to the lobby, the tall tree had been cut down about a foot . . . from the top. Enough to accommodate the menorah, which then had been ingeniously wired to stay secured at the very top of the tree, thereby having the menorah representing the eight days of Chanukah doing double duty as the star atop the Christmas tree. The staff had to pull out the ladder to add a bulb for each day of Chanukah.

27

Encroachments and Entitlements

My own experience with property entitlement started with a perceived privet encroachment. It started when the privet was planted at Paul's and my house in Southampton. Someone I had never met before called me, screaming. It took a few moments to calm the stranger down and find out who was so upset and why. It turned out to be one of our neighbors. The young, straggly shrub was blocking her view of my yard. A few weeks later, we installed a pool fence on her side of the hedge. She called again, screaming even louder this time about how ugly it was and that we should move the fence to our side of the hedge, even though the fence was legally on our side of the property line. Typically, most neighbors in Southampton put the required pool fence on the property line, sharing in the cost; then they each put in a row of privet for maximum privacy. I assured her that soon the privet would grow through the fence and she would not even see it. A year later, she and her husband put in a pool. As they had brought the level of their yard higher, the pool fence was no longer at the legal height on their side. Without a word to us, they had several inches of fencing added to our fence. We had no problem with it, though it would have been nice had they put privet on their side of the pool fence as well.

A few weeks before we had our pool put in, we had two fairly large trees planted near our privet hedge. They were for shade, but also to block the neighbors' windows that looked over the privet and into our yard. The tree guys were looking around and rolling their eyes. We could all hear yelling from the other side of the now ten-foot, solid green wall, "Don't take my sun, don't take my sun, oh please, don't take my sun." No one knew what was really going on till she came marching over, with hubby in tow, to demand we not put those trees in. I tried to reason with her. She had gotten over the privet and the pool fence; hopefully she would get over the trees.

For even more privacy, we put in arborvitae along the side of the patio. We ordered them the same day she mentioned her daughter was having a baby and she was going out of town to help for two weeks. When she returned, she told Paul she loved them. We were surprised, but several months later would learn why. They had not wanted privet because of the work involved in maintaining them, but they approved of the arborvitae because there was less upkeep. Ironically, we had decided not to pull out all the privet in favor of having all arborvitae because these neighbors had contributed so much to the privet maturing, which needs constant pruning and which they had done on their side.

A few other events occurred. While working on the corner of the pool house, a neighbor called to complain that we were putting pool equipment too close to their property. The village building department sent someone over to see if we had noise making pool pumps too close to the property line. We were not installing any equipment, but merely had dug a hole in order to pull electrical wires into the pool house. Our pool equipment was already installed in the basement of the pool house. Next, we heard there were complaints about one of Paul's construction trucks parked on the street for a few hours, which was followed by being shut down for building the overhang on our patio, which was described in our permit but was not in our original plans. Since we had been building on and off for so long, we had forgotten that we had yet to determine exactly what material we wanted at the outset, and so the overhang hadn't been included. We took the required four directional photos and had Terry draw up plans. We then raced to the building department to submit the papers before the deadline in order to get in front of the next monthly Architectural Village Review Board meeting, essentially the Village of Southampton's version of a co-op board. Fortunately, the folks at the building department really liked Paul. He was the only Texan builder in town. They also loved making fun of how long we were taking with our personal project. They were all laughing when we came in.

"Hey," Cliff said, "I was in my forties when you guys started! I had my fiftieth birthday, what a year after you started."

"Yeah, and he just turned fifty-one this week!" one of the office ladies added, laughing even louder.

Cliff looked delighted as he shared the next bit of news. "You just missed your neighbor, who came in to complain that your hedges are too high." He laughed, and the whole office joined in. "We would have loved to watch a fistfight over that one." There were a few more chuckles all around, and we couldn't help but laugh along with them, because just that morning, we had seen someone had cut into our hedges, creating an awful-looking step at the top. Hedges are meant to be straight up and straight across. There are hedge specialists who use laser beams and piano wires to get perfect ninety-degree angles. Some of the larger homes have bills over $100,000 for one season's clippings. Ours now had one side a foot and a half shorter than the other.

I mentioned this to Cliff.

"That's against the law!" he exclaimed. "You can sue. There are more lawsuits over hedges in the Hamptons than any other infraction."

One of the other guys recited the law to us: One may trim the side of the hedges that might infringe on your own side. *You may only trim hedges that are not growing on your property in a straight line from the ground to the sky.*

This news gave me an idea.

That afternoon, plans for our overhang in hand, we paid our neighbors a visit. At first the wife, who answered the front door, hedged (get it?) on our request for a five-minute chat. I walked to the backyard, where her husband was mowing, while Paul contended with her as she screamed after me, "You can't have everything you want, missy!"

My intention was not to create tension but to disarm the situation. It was a very successful meeting. They aired their complaints; we aired ours; then I suggested we find those areas we could each compromise on. They would have their too-loud air-conditioning compressor fixed, and we promised to install whisper-quiet compressors. They would adjust a bright light that pierced through to our pool house, and we would trim the hedges lower. I had never considered that the husband was concerned about having to climb so high to keep their side trimmed. While I didn't think they looked old at all, they mentioned that they were and were fearful about climbing ladders. We offered to trim their side whenever we trimmed the rest, mentioning the hedge law that also required written permission to go on your neighbor's side for such trim time. The wife mentioned what a good job her husband was doing and that he would continue. I told her that we had already thinned out the trees, and each season we would continue to do so, so as not to block all her sun. She seemed to accept that as a partial concession and pointed out that the roots would grow into her yard one day.

Okay, I could understand her concerns: they were about aging and the ease of their future retirement. Would the roots cause harm to their lovely, bluestone patio, or their foundation? We showed them the drawings we had submitted and explained that we had no plans to use the roof as a second-floor sundeck, no longer permitted in Southampton as one might then be able to see over the hedges, into your neighbor's yard. The husband had no problem with the plan and said he would come to the review board meeting but would not raise any objections.

One part of my mind wondered how he put up with her complaining, but my next thought was how we all react to change. Sometimes we resist until we see that it's not so bad. I found myself liking them and hoping they would one day visit for drinks . . . when we were finally done with everything. Their biggest complaint was how long they had lived with our endless construction, and they were right, even though Paul always took noise into consideration and tried to be a good neighbor.

"You know," I said to her, "our houses are so close we're practically roommates. Let's communicate with each other, rather than run to the village to complain." They both agreed. A few nights later, we saw them waiting for a table at one of our favorite restaurants. He was standing up a step, on the deck, and she was looking up at him, and he leaned over and tenderly kissed her on the lips. My heart melted—they reminded me of my mother and father, a husband who still saw the young, beautiful woman he married.

28

The Five Buyer
Negotiating Styles

With our years in real estate, Alfred and I have ascertained that there are five distinct negotiating styles when it comes to purchasing a property. Sniffers and circlers, hunters, hedgers, bottom-feeders, and bargainers.

Many who move to New York City have heard that New Yorkers are rough and rude, and that the brokers here are sharks, and so they are well prepared to defend their understandable position. We would like to point out a few quirks of our social graces, which anyone hunting for real estate in New York City should soon adopt. First, what appears to be discourtesy is really that we are moving fast and looking to maximize your time and ours. Second, we also talk fast—if we are actually talking, because the whole world is texting. The key here is short and to the point. Sometimes you might just have to pick up the phone for effective communication and do business the old-fashioned way. Amazingly, you can cover a lot more with a few quick spoken words versus long texts. Last, our personal space is at a minimum, so bumping shoulders, or even bumpers, is no cause to stop and take time for apologies or exchange insurance information. Everyone keeps on moving.

These interactive habits are a part of the fiber of negotiations, no matter what kind of a negotiator you might identify as. Some might see themselves as a combination of two or three, or one may start out one way and transition into another. Different cultures bring in different perspectives and styles of negotiating. For us, all are acceptable.

Sniffers and Circlers

Sniffers and circlers keep looking and trying on different properties. They must know every available home, not only in their parameters, but also the entire inventory. Some enter negotiations using this tack; they first want to know if anyone else has bid. They will go to the open houses and stay through the entire two or three hours to see if any other buyers are showing interest or whispering to the listing broker. They bring multiple friends and family to the property over the course of days and even weeks, should the home be on the market for a while. This in itself is cause for more sniffing, because why hasn't someone else wanted it? Some sniffers and circlers can circle for years. When ready to bid, they are diligent. They think and sniff some more before responding to counteroffers. To their detriment, the time they take to negotiate could cause them to miss out when a more aggressive negotiator, say a hunter, comes along. But when they commit, they commit.

Having started out as sniffers and circlers, Alfred and I didn't miss a house when we were searching for the perfect tax exchange Southampton property. We drove in loops for weeks and scanned every listing online and in the papers, sniffing out every possibility, going to every open house no matter the price (as education about the market and future expansion possibilities), and engaging a local broker to help navigate the best deal. We tried on lots of houses and waited for the right opportunity. Now for us, as soon as we identified our prey, we deftly transitioned into hunters. To be a successful negotiating hunter, your M.O. is to forget the sniffing. In other words, it's time to focus and strategize the win.

Hunters

Hunters waste no time. They find out who the best are in the area they want to purchase in, then quickly winnow down to an aggressive broker, most likely whoever was quickest on the draw, responding to their email first. In contrast to the sniffers and circlers, they do not want to see everything on the market and are very precise in describing their desires. Hunters expect their brokers to show them the best, finely curated properties and spreadsheets on comparable units, including an analysis of price per square foot, positives and negatives, possible costs for upgrades, and suggested bid levels. When the crosshairs are lined up, they pull the trigger and bid to show the owner they mean business. They also test the owner's negotiability by submitting the initial offer low enough not to appear anxious but high enough not to look like a bottom-feeder. The hunter is aimed at a good property priced correctly. Following the owner's counteroffer, hunters swiftly go in for the kill, increasing their offer to a fair price with terms that include a deadline for the owner to accept it.

Hedgers

Hedgers make unemotional overtures on several properties before bidding and will make offers on all properties that make it to their preferred list. Then they will make a decision, based on value. This is not common, as most people feel it's not right to place bids on more than one property; conversely, many sellers entertain multiple offers—an offer is no guarantee of a deal. Even an offer that has been accepted is no guarantee. Hedgers feel that what's good for the goose is good for the gander, and we respect that. Hedgers will not be left empty-handed, having placed bids on more than one option.

Bottom-Feeders

The bottom-feeders search for properties that have been lingering on the market, sometimes because they have extremely poor design decisions that are costly to fix. Not everyone appreciates green granite for all the floors in an apartment, or the washer installed above a toilet. One of my personal favorites was a one-bedroom condo where an entire corner of the living room had a floor-to-ceiling built-in glass terrarium for a pet boa constrictor. Really unfortunate views, like the parking lot of a restaurant where overflowing dumpsters are visible, will greatly diminish a sales price. And so these properties may appeal to the bottom-feeder looking for a deal, often for the purpose of changing or hiding the offending features and then reselling for a tidy profit. Bottom-feeders can smell an old listing but are most interested in rooting out desperate situations by putting in ultra-low offers until getting a bite. To reach closing, they must perceive the property to be substantially below market value. They will point out all the reasons why a property is only worth the low number they are offering. They have no allegiance to any broker or property. Some even put out their own ads and send email blasts that say, "All cash will close immediately," expecting to find the absolute best deal, even if the property is a real dog. On the other hand, when they sell, they price way over market and scoff at anything that is not full ask.

Bargainers

The bargainers will only buy direct from the listing broker and even prefer to find owners selling without a professional. If there is a listing broker, bargainers are known for insisting the commission be half, claiming they are representing themselves. They make offers with all kinds of unusual terms, and when all the terms are met, they add some more. Should the next round of terms be met, even more terms are added. Bargainers see extreme negotiating as a sporting experience, so expecting an owner to throw in the sconces, and maybe even the beds, is part of the competition and adrenaline high. They can't part with their money unless they feel the rush of taking full advantage of an opportunity, and there is nothing wrong with that. Even at closing, they have the unique ability to find something to turn to their advantage and are fond of a last-minute negotiation tool: threatening not to close. A bargainer attorney is always employed and participates in the "I'll walk away" gambit to gain a few more dollars or a bit more chattel at closing. To be a successful bargainer, you need chutzpah—and a great poker face.

We admire all five and all combinations of negotiating styles.

29

New York Party Time

We Rennas get along really well with Lenora, another top broker who left Corcoran when Alfred did. One time she and her husband at the time decided to hold a party, the venue of which changed three times. Three times, updated invitations were sent out. A lot of people were dazed and confused. Not us. Another time they were hosting a VIP sit-down dinner out in Southampton that included heads of state, banks, and other organizations. They had four people send last-minute cancellations due to some country's unrest. In one hour, all four of us were dressed and ready to dine using our most diplomatic manners, charm, and up-to-the-minute world-event knowledge. By the second course, we had everyone relaxed and laughing. Were we insulted that we were not on the guest list months before? Not at all. Just like when some people have a date sprout up even when they already have plans and they dump the friends to take the date, as brokers, we're used to having to change plans all the time. A buyer or seller calls, and no matter who else awaits, wait they must.

Back to the Manhattan party, which was to celebrate the arrival of their second child. Alfred and I arrived early, as we both had other events on our agendas for that evening. From the moment the first cork popped, he and I were rooted at the French doors from the entry foyer to the living room, within perfect view of the front door. Every time it opened, we heard one of two refrains: "Oh, you look fabulous" or, "Oh, look, there're the Rennas!" We were like the second welcoming committee, standing with friends we thought of as adopted siblings. The champagne flowed, the tidbits were tasty, and we were happily sipping and nibbling.

All of the Renna clan was included, and it was a perfect real estate event: Fifth Avenue, prewar Classic Six, Central Park view, birds swooping in patterns against the setting sun, its sunlight filling the rooms and twinkling off clinking crystal stemware and bejeweled guests. Our champagne glasses were perpetually topped off with a fizzing, pink potion accompanied by miniscule yet decadent hors d'oeuvres. There were thimble-sized morsels of mac and cheese with lobster and truffles, and miniature crepe cones dusted with pepper and oozing with smoked salmon and crème fraîche. Other impressive delights included perfectly manicured lamb chops, the offering of which required two magnificent servers attired in perfectly starched, white Nehru jackets, one offering the little skeleton parts from a silver tray, the other awaiting your remains with another sterling vessel.

Accompanying the chattering mix of New York power brokers, heiresses, bankers, and famously single doctors was a Julliard string trio. The guest of honor, whom we all came to meet, was their six-pound baby boy, held before all like an offering by the uniformed baby nurse. The mother, sleek in an ice-blue, shimmering sheath, looked slim and stunning. "Oh, isn't she a vision of ice blue," sneered someone standing nearby, who turned out to be the jealous partner of the hostess's best friend.

"Oh, yes," Alfred said, proud of our friend and ignoring the nasty undertone, "and to think, she gave birth less than four weeks ago."

"I heard she had a glass of wine, delivered the baby, took the weekend off, and was back in the office on Monday." Another broker standing with us said in awe.

"She threw this party just to show off her figure."

"I bet she's got several pairs of Spanx on under that gorgeous shmata."

"I accidently brushed against her to check—she's Spanx free."

We turned from the gossipers to continue our much more interesting conversation with a distinguished gentleman who had cornered us.

"He was definitely in our personal space," Alfred said when we left, bearing in mind "personal space" is already greatly cut down at a New York cocktail party.

The parties of that evening continued with an opening at a Madison Avenue gallery with famous models and a pop-up gallery owner. The sidewalk decor included red carpet, velvet ropes, an overweight bouncer in a black suit, and a thin gallery gal in a black dress holding a clipboard with the guest list. Now, anyone can get past this setup because at art openings, they want as many people as they can fit in the gallery. Mr. Gallery Owner, who has lots of hedge-fund money to spend on hype, had hired dozens of models to come, plus a quick $50,000 appearance by a rap artist who has not rapped a live performance in years. A few more dollars bought guys with heavy-looking cameras and long lenses, giving everyone the sense that they were rich and famous. The average height of the guests, with the towering platform heels, was six foot six. In a moment, Donna and Janney, a close friend and broker who met up with us at the first party, who averaged about five foot two between them, were lost in a sea of legs. It was like pushing through an overgrown jungle to find them and move on to our next event.

Alfred had gone in the opposite direction, to a fundraiser dedicated to promoting the arts in public schools and honoring some famous artists, such as Christo—who likes to hang curtains in various inconvenient places such as across the Grand Canyon, or wrapping up islands like he did in the Caribbean—whom we greatly admire. Manhattan even had our own installation called *Gates*, where the paths of Central Park featured thousands of Hermés-orange flags that went all the way around Central Park. Alfred's invite was to an event in an eight-thousand-square-foot loft.

"As I meandered through the loft," Alfred related to me the next morning, "to admire the multimillion-dollar art collection, the lovely hostess caught up with me to warn me not to go out to the north terrace, where there were boxes full of bees."

"Bees?" I asked.

Alfred laughed. "'I thought I was looking at an art installation,' I told her. 'Why are there bees at this height and in the city?' I asked her, as I peered through the wall of glass like it was a diorama at the Museum of Natural History. She proceeded to tell me all about how bees, vital to our ecosystem, were vanishing. Her tiny guests produce a hundred of pounds of honey on a semiannual basis. It was very impressive. The proceeds, of course, go to a foundation to save the honey bees."

"Wow. I think it's the most unselfish thing to offer a million-dollar terrace to host bees." I put honey in my tea every morning, not to mention it is a travesty to lose any part of our bee population.

"This owner was happy to accommodate the beekeeper and the bees, and is compensated with two jars of honey for each crop. Oh, and she has another even larger south-facing terrace."

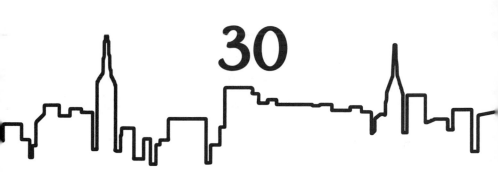

30

Field of Dreams and Top of the Mountain: NYC's Determined Buyers

Alphas

The field of buyer types is broad here, on this spit of an island that sits in the streams of two massive rivers. One prominent type of buyer is the alpha male; Alphas thrive in high-stakes maneuvering. They start out as hunters and prefer not to circle a postwar home unless it has lots of bedrooms and is a penthouse with a huge terrace, in which case it becomes a trophy property in a plebian building. A potential apartment must be a full floor in a large enough building to have at least 6000 square feet, or high-ceilinged duplex, dripping with moldings; a prewar spread that includes four wood-burning fireplaces, living room, library, formal dining room, and master bedroom suite. In addition, it must have three maids' rooms counted in the twelve- to eighteen-room spread; great city, river, or park views; and the prospect that some clever bargainer-style negotiating will get it for a steal. These hunters are expert at turning up clues as to a seller's motivations and probable negotiability. I had an alpha buyer who perfectly fit this pattern.

Dale—tall, handsome, and brilliant—could read an entire document upside down on someone's desk and remember every single word. I know—I witnessed it. We were looking at a great condo when I saw him peer at a contract in the seller's study. About all I caught was that it was for the purchase of another condo because it said in large cap letters across the top: CONTRACT OF SALE CONDOMINIUM UNIT. Dale later related the address, unit number, sales price, monthly charges, purchaser's LLC, his attorney's name, address, phone number, and email. He saw acquired information as vital to the negotiating process.

When Dale was ready to bid, he had chosen a second-choice property and bid on both, using the second as a hedge but mostly for negotiating balance. Here are the clues that Dale had entered his perfect apartment. He morphed into a sniffer and circler, stalking about alone, though he expected me, his broker, and the listing broker to be within earshot should he have a question. He chose a couple of choice spots to sit down. I could see him envisioning having an evening cocktail or a morning protein shake. Then he asked who else was looking at the property. I watched him when we first arrived, spying a piece of mail in the foyer followed by him discreetly sending a text to his assistant to start a search and see if there was evidence that the seller was having financial or marital issues, or pending legal action that would help him figure out the best approach. I know because when we left, he told what he learned.

A young, pretty, Ivy League graduate often accompanies the super-rich Alpha, regardless of his age, and she anticipates quitting her job to have more time for Pilates and to accommodate her future husband's schedule, become a mother, and sit on a board or two for philanthropic causes. The male wants his female to recognize his prowess and to be recognized as having found the *trophy property* they are entitled to. The lady of the future abode will allow him this conquest—after all, she will be getting the bigger bathroom and one of the four or five bedrooms as her closet. Dale followed the pattern exquisitely, showing up at the second round of looking at properties with his beautiful future bride.

Alpha Betas

This is a powerful and growing group—our female Alphas are extraordinarily successful, do not have time to waste, and know exactly what they want. If they are sending a surrogate to do their previewing, it won't be a mother, admin, boy toy, or boyfriend; it will be their trusted decorator who will narrow down the search to only those properties that meet all expectations and needs, and who will study every floor plan and taken copious notes and photos. Fortunate to have a customer who will also always be loyal, the experienced broker must be able to negotiate appointments with listing brokers sans customer. When the motivated customer shows up, she will inspect the potential property, already familiar with all aspects of the plan and what her decorator is advising for renovations and decor. As a listing broker, I once had only the broker and decorator come to the apartment. The buyer did not set foot in the condominium until every last towel and roll of toilet paper was in place. It's worthy of mention that she had seven other homes and a full-time home manager.

Unlike the Alpha, the Alpha Beta does not need to sniff, circle, hunt, or puff up her chest, nor does she have to sit and imagine herself puffing a cigar before the fire—and all the closets will be hers.

Alpha–Alpha Betas

These are a powerhouse of dueling couples. The Alpha–Alpha Betas, who each have a powerful financial position, feel they are entitled to a trophy property. They are a growling, prowling, fine set of species of true hunters; however, they do not have time to run around and preview properties themselves, so they designate one or even both of their moms to preview apartments for them, along with their star architect and decorator. They shun prewar apartments. They want a home where no one has gone before.

The Affluent Buyer

The Affluent Buyer has a sense of earned entitlement. It has taken them decades to accumulate their wealth, and they are quietly proud of their accomplishments. The Affluent Buyer wants a realtor who will expedite their property search, pulling all of the various pieces together. This means winnowing down the best choices, but also expecting the broker to provide a very high level of service that starts with the first impression—being prompt, professionally and well attired, and able to anticipate their needs. These buyers know in a moment whether a property will work for them. The broker should recognize when it does not and cut the visit short.

Affluent Buyers may be male or female, and often come in pairs, having chosen their mates well, sharing living expenses, and not necessarily having children. They will speak of the need for art walls and wall washers, and are very happy to find a home where another owner has already done the work. Almost all will discuss corners where they might put their Eames lounge and ottoman, or in the case of a couple, their twin set of Eames. The Affluent Buyers read and collect hardcover books, and especially love signed first additions, so abundant bookcases are a big selling point.

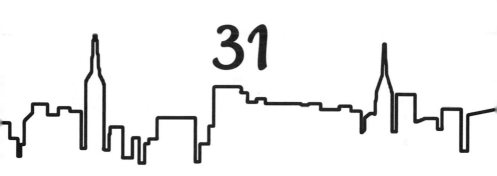

31

Bag of Frozen Peas

A year and a half had passed since our father had died, and we were still hanging on to our family home. It was a convenient detour when heading to or from Southampton on the Long Island Expressway. We all were stopping to use the bathroom, maybe make a cup of coffee, and putter around to consider which items we could use. Anything we took, we'd immediately report to the others via text.

> I'd like the old percolator coffee pot if no else does
> Take it
> K

A couple of weeks after dad's funeral, I stopped at the Little Neck house feeling a bit hungry for something sweet and some good coffee.

I dug out my personal stash of favorite coffee beans from behind the liquor bottles and used our father's grinder. While I waited for the water to boil, I opened the freezer, hoping that someone else may have left behind a muffin or something similar. The only thing I found was an old package of frozen peas.

Back when our mother broke the news to each of us, one at a time, that our parents had sold our family summer home with all its contents, I was hopping around in a cast, recovering from a bicycle accident that had occurred soon after I graduated from college. She and I were in the kitchen preparing dinner, and I had just yanked open the broken freezer drawer when she blurted the news to me. My immediate tears had dropped onto a package of frozen peas. It was devastating to lose our most special place and the things we loved. She had sent Alfred a letter to break the news to him. He was spending a semester of college in Rome, paid for with money he had saved up.

I looked through the glass of the backdoor to the back porch. I remembered feeling like a fish out of water in the summers after we sold the beach house. That first summer, trying to fill our idle days, Alfred and I made our own backgammon board. We found scrap wood in the garage and sawed, sanded, measured, taped, painted, and trimmed. I could barely sleep till we had saved enough money from our part-time jobs and finally bought a set of stone checkers. It wasn't long before our neighborhood friends came around, some with their own boards, and we all spent hours playing, multiple games going, late into the hot city nights. The sound of crickets was comforting, even if we could hear the hum of the expressway.

The water boiled, and I slowly poured it over the fragrant grinds. Before our father died, I'd make both of us a cup of coffee while he called off the choices of something sweet that he kept in the freezer. "Mmm, Jo, how about a nice piece of pound cake warmed up, with some chocolate ice cream?"

Three years had passed since our parents sold our summer home before we finally learned why they had to. Our father had embarked on a business venture in a mining business that had left him in financial ruins. That desperate time eventually caused our mother to have a nervous breakdown. When she recovered, our father collapsed from the weight of so much emotional damage. We kids had become the earners and caregivers. While I should have been ready to launch my own life and new career, I remained at home. The losses would haunt each of us for many years.

Millie and Al did eventually get back on their feet. Our father started a business of medical technology research that created staggering piles of notes, a vast assortment of research, and dozens of copies of his published books. All this was added to files of decades-old drawings from his aeronautics engineering career, along with his classified files that were no longer government secrets, fascinating photographs from surveillance planes, and other aviation engineering projects he had worked on.

All of this stuff that represented his life overflowed to other areas of the house. Our mother, whose true love and talent was interior design, had been his research assistant. She hated the dry work and all the stuff she considered clutter. But together, they got their life back to normal, and were able to keep their Little Neck house and do a little traveling. I was twenty-seven when I finally felt it was okay for me to leave home and move into my own apartment in the city.

After a number of unfulfilling jobs, I realized I was choosing areas that most closely resembled my father's idea of women's careers. His ideal that women were meant to be barefoot and pregnant—which was in such contrast to how he had supported our childhood building project—pushed me away from motherhood. I was also intent on being able to take care of myself, whether or not I had a man in my life—unlike my mother, who felt like she never had use of her own money. That's when I began my quest to develop a business that would eventually enable me to buy, sell, and build properties of my own. My first entrepreneurial attempts were failures. Then one day, I saw an ad to be a real estate agent. I had been living on my own long enough that I didn't feel guilty about going against my father's wishes. Each of his children had reacted to the events of our youth, most especially to the loss of our summer home, in similar ways, and it all came down to real estate.

In 1985, Rosemary was the first to buy a house in Southampton. It had taken coerciveness and planning for her to convince the man who would become her husband that he could have a lucrative medical practice in Southampton, rather than be an employee of an existing medical office in a small, faraway town called Elmira. By the time Rosemary set up her husband's practice, including purchasing and renovating a professional building, and was ready to renovate their house, my husband, Jonathan, and I had bought a weekend home far from the Hamptons, which he wanted no part of. It was an 1850s farmhouse in upstate New York, which we eventually sold to build our dream house on the remaining thirty-eight acres of that property. To my father's great delight, our home was near where he had gone in the summers as a young boy, and my parents spent many weekends with us, as they did at Alfred's and Rosemary's. At about the time Jonathan and I first purchased, Alfred bought his house in Southampton a short walk from Rosemary's. I was determined to eventually get there, and so was Donna.

Thinking about all this, I walked around the house with my mug of coffee, having given up on finding a muffin or an old tin of cookies. I went down to the basement to assess how much work we had ahead of us. Hanging in the closets were winter clothes, all kinds of heavy coats, and our father's army uniforms. No one really wanted them, but none of us knew what to do with them. There were only two stories we heard about our father's military service, and both were about how our father's life had been spared during World War II. The first was when he was removed from a ship just before it was sent to Pearl Harbor. The second was when he was on an alternating flight schedule for army planes, one day on, one day off.

One morning, he woke up vomiting. His counterpart offered to trade places with him for the next day. The plane crashed and all aboard perished. While he did not lose life or limb, he lost other aspects of himself. Our father was extremely secretive, and this was one of the only life experiences he had shared with us, and so it was the only thing we could attribute as the cause for him to lose his ability to laugh, reason, and negotiate, despite his genius mind. We had to struggle to find our own commerce and negotiating abilities. Our mother and we four kids never struggled to find humor. We all inherited the best of our parents' talents: our father's engineering mind and our mother's eye for fine design and desire to create beautiful homes. My inability to push against my father's idea that only men should be architects rerouted my architectural desires into design urges, and there aren't enough websites or open houses to quench it. Most important, we all inherited our mother's gift of laughter.

I went back up to the kitchen, where so much of our lives had been lived. I looked out the window and saw that the birdbath was dry. I filled a pot and went out to replenish the water. Watching the birds play was one of the things my mother enjoyed. As I washed my mug, I realized we were all ready to let go. It was time to get Little Neck in selling condition and put it on the market, and the first order of business was to have a dumpster delivered.

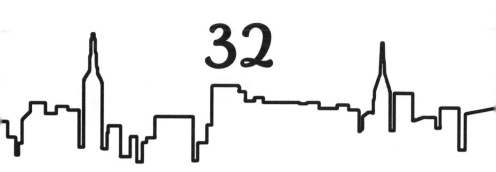

32

The Sabbath Apartment

Fair housing laws don't allow us to describe an apartment as being a "great family home." Describing any attributes of a property in a way that directly relates to what families look for discriminates against single people and people who are without children, and is not permitted by fair housing laws. You also cannot say "steps from the park" or "near playground," which discriminates against people with physical disabilities, though we can say "one block from the park or playground" which is not considered an opinion but a fact about distance and therefore not discriminatory.

The customer attracted to a three- or four-bedroom apartment is often living with a partner, married or not, and has at least a couple of children living with them. Being one and three quarters of a block from a playground is a plus in these situations. Anyway, these folks will often make compromise to either go for a smaller high floor apartment with lots of light, (light being a premium), or go for a larger apartment (space being the premium), on a lower floor, and most likely at a lower price. Of course we are speaking of buildings with elevators, the opposite being true for walk-up buildings, where the price goes down as you go up.

While fair housing laws also protect against religious discrimination, a low floor is perfect for Sabbath-observant Jewish people. For some, pressing an elevator button on the Sabbath is considered work and hence a sin. The alternative is to take the stairs, and a low floor is certainly desirable in that case. There is added value in a building that is only a few blocks to the nearest temple and where the elevators are programed to automatically stop on each and every floor from sundown on Friday to sundown on Saturday and on all holy days. The added value decreases if there is not a second elevator, fondly known as the express, for those owners who may press the elevator button without consequence.

In all cases, it is the proximity of these buildings, fair housing or no, to certain kinds of institutions—whether religious or educational, whether private or public—as well as places that are surrounded by grass and have amenities where people (and pets if permitted) of all ages can roll, run, walk, stand, sit, swing, or slide, that is desirable.

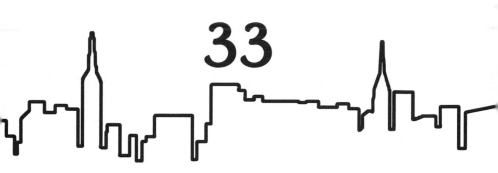

33

Time to Say Good-Bye

We four siblings unanimously agreed it was time to prepare the family home for sale. The first order of business was to get the largest dumpster that would fit on the driveway. That first weekend with the dumpster, to our surprise, a whole new world of farming for listings opened to us. *Farming* is a term used in real estate to refer to the practice of knocking on doors or sending out mailers in a neighborhood where a broker would like to find new listings. It was like we put out a Vegas-style billboard inviting anyone with any service to ring our bell. In the city, a dumpster means an old building is coming down and a new one is going up. In the suburbs, it screams, "Estate!" It is apparently a casting call for brokers and all other suburban experts to show up and sing the praises of their services. The doorbell rang like it was Halloween. One day, when Rosemary and I had the front door propped open to throw stuff from up on the front porch into the dumpster down on the driveway, we found someone roaming around the house looking for price tags. They thought we were the tag sale company.

One of my favorite unexpected service sellers stopped by when Rosemary and I decided, after filling several ten-yard dumpsters and various U-Hauls and pickup trucks, we were ready to stage the house and the yard. I was scraping up big patches of moss that had carpeted the back steps when I said, "We need someone to power wash all the brick facade and outside staircases. Moss is growing everywhere." A moment later, the doorbell rang. It was a man who "did everything." So we asked if he power washed, and he said that power washing was his specialty. We invited him to start immediately and left him to do his thing while we took off for the craft store, Michaels, where we purchased artificial flowers for the planters and a couple of tubes of acrylic paint we intended on mixing for the kitchen cabinets. By the time we returned, all the brick and stone looked fabulous. The house gleamed.

"Those were artificial flowers outside?" Alfred exclaimed after he went by the house a few days later. There was no way to water unless one of us drove to Little Neck every single day. After we put in the colorful plastic flowers and trailing vines, Rosemary took the moss patches and topped off each planter. We even watered them for a realistic look. By nightfall, we still had to touch up the years of chipped paint on the kitchen cabinets. It wasn't till the next time we stopped by and it was daylight that we saw the color was not the perfect match we had thought. Instead, the cabinets were striated. Delightfully, it looked new and interesting. I heard the new owners kept them just as they were. But it was all a lot of work, which led to how we hired a local broker.

On the first day of August, we had set a self-imposed deadline of the first Sunday after Labor Day to have our first open house, planning for two of us to alternate each week. We were not looking forward to it even though we're all brokers and know what to do. The Sunday before Labor Day, Alfred and I were on final cleanup duty, and he sauntered down the block where Shula, a local broker, was having an open house. He invited her to stop by, and Shula came in with a portfolio filled with her successes, sold us with her Greek accent, enthusiasm, and assurance to work hard. Plus she promised to bring Greek cookies next time we were at the house. We signed her exclusive right on the spot and headed back to the city tremendously relieved.

We could never have done what Shula did. She had open houses every Saturday and Sunday besides showing it all week long. The only thing she did, which was contrary to most broker/seller situations, was to advise an asking price higher than we had decided on. Maybe she wanted to impress us. For Shula, it was important that the price have as many eights as possible; as she explained, it would make the house more attractive to Asian buyers, who believe that eight is a fortuitous number.

We tested the waters for two weeks. We knew momentum was key to getting the highest price, and we asked Shula to drop the ask quickly, before the listing became shop worn. At the new price and with a few suggestions about how to show it from us, it sold immediately to a sweet, young couple. They wanted to close as soon as possible. It was time to remove the last of the furnishings we'd used to make the house lovely and welcoming. Our mother would have been thrilled at how beautiful it looked. I suspect she would not have minded that it took us nearly two years before we were ready to say good-bye.

I had thought it would be good karma to leave our mother's favorite garden urns, birdbath, and a Japanese lantern as part of the sale, even though it would be sad not to see them anymore. They had each given her so much pleasure. Each had been thoughtfully and strategically placed. The lantern peeked out from a thick bed of ivy, beneath a soaring maple tree in the backyard. The birdbath was tucked between two arching hedges, so the birds felt safe, and the planting urns flanked the rear patio.

All had years of beautiful patina. Since we all still detour off the highway to pass by our old home, we have watched as its new family has taken on a home project of their own—creating a rock garden in the front yard. They have built a low wall with pink, scalloped bricks and filled in over the lawn with pink pebbles. All of our mother's garden things—the urns, birdbath, and lantern—have been placed right there in front, where we can see them whenever we drive by.

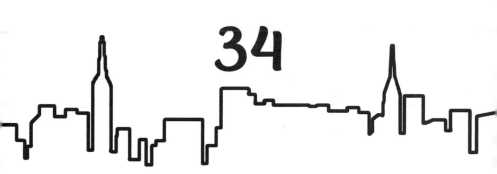

34

Self-Informed and Savvy Sellers

There are basically two types of sellers: those who trust a professional and those who believe they know more than the professionals. Within those categories, there are the sellers who say they are not in hurry and believe the longer their home is on the market the more money they'll get. But they can always turn into the next subcategory: sellers who are, for whatever reasons, desperate to sell.

A realtor with history will have referrals and buyers who become their sellers. There is trust already built in, and the wise seller looks to us to take the lead. There are six basic aspects that make for a successful sale: timing, pricing, staging, marketing, negotiating, and closing. Within this is the all-important—momentum, from the moment the trigger is pulled. As many of us say, "You are out of the gate only once." The savvy seller knows that, as a listing gets old, it gets stale, and no one wants a stale listing unless it's for a steal. The untrusting seller hurts themselves when they either rely only on their own information or allow fear to affect their decision-making, and loss is the end result.

Toward the end of 2014, we had an owner approach us to rent his ten-room duplex condominium. It had very special protected views over landmarked town houses and historical gardens. We determined a rental price, and he added $7,000 per month to that number, claiming he had just recently gotten that. We said we'd try, but after two weeks, it would be wise to drop the price. During the course of attempting to find a tenant for the overpriced rental, the owner decided to sell the unit instead. We regrouped, suggesting that the apartment needed to be painted and the floors refinished. Since he lived in Vegas, he asked if we could find someone to do the work. We did. Next, he wisely decided to have the main rooms staged. Again, we made ourselves available for numerous visits to the apartment. It did look quite nice in spite of all the work it needed, and our photos and marketing materials were beautiful. We had priced the unit at $9.1 million. The owner decided to make the ask $10.5 million. Again, we agreed he would lower the price after two weeks if we had no serious interest. It was now early 2015. Large apartments were accumulating on the market in both rentals and sales. For Uptown where this unit was located, the average listings over $9 million had been hovering at about forty on the market at any given point over the last five years. But new condos were being built at a rapid pace, most in the over-$9 million price range, and hundreds were coming to a completion over the course of the following eighteen months. The prior robust market also motivated many sellers to put their apartments on the market at higher and higher numbers. Other factors were causing the absorption rate to slow down: national debt and new government disclosure laws over real estate purchases by LLCs and corporations that had been meant to hide the identity of the owners.

In addition, foreign countries, such as China, Russia, and India, were limiting the amount of money their citizens could take out of their country (much of which had previously gone into real estate investments in New York), coupled with the declining value of the euro. Even units considered hot and guaranteed to sell with multiple offers were sitting longer without bids.

I sent our client the list of available apartments for $9 million and up. There were 243 and counting. He continued to stick to his price. Another thing brokers like to say is, "Your first offer is your highest offer." It is almost always true. Right at the beginning, we had a couple willing to pay $8.5 million. They did not want to negotiate, since they thought the asking price was out of line, but were ready to sign on the dotted line with their offer. His response was that he would not even entertain anything that did not have a 9 in front of it. As time went on, he finally agreed to come down to $9.8 million, then $9.4 million, then $9.2 million. The problem was, he was still too high and merely chasing the tide out.

Toward the end of our exclusive term, we had two firm offers, one at $6.5 million and another at $6.7 million, both all cash. The owner turned those down, though they were in pace with the new reality of declining prices. He was holding on for a reverse in trend, though there were no indicators that it would happen. Our listing agreement expired, and he went on to hire a new firm.

Within a week, we had a new exclusive listing in the same building, with the same view, only a higher, better floor. It was very fortuitous for us. Our new owner, with whom we had done business before, trusted our numbers. In fact, we had come in within a few dollars of the appraisal they had done for estate planning. We contacted the buyers we had met on the overpriced unit to see if they would be interested in the new listing. It was basically the same layout, two rooms smaller at the back of the unit, but an extra room had been added at the front, creating a fantastic, expansive living room. One of the couples jumped on it. Both they and our owners traded counter-offers fairly, and we consummated a sale and had a signed contract four days after listing. We had several backup offers as well. By that time, we saw that our previous client, who had insisted he knew the market better than we did, had drastically dropped his asking price. The last time we checked, it had finally sold at $6,050,000, below all of the bids he had turned down. Unfortunately, self-informed sellers who believe they know more than the experts or who are blinded by the idea that somehow their apartment is better than anything else are also the last to see a changing market, most especially when prices are on the decline.

At times, we deal with sellers who are pressured to sell. If it's financial stress, as in the following example, it could lead to a desperate situation. We had a client who had signed a contract for a house in the suburbs and were hoping their apartment would be an easy sell. Fortunately, they priced right where we suggested, and immediately, we had two buyers bidding on their co-op. One bid was considerably higher than the other. The concern was the board application. In the sellers' final decision, knowing that the buyers' brokers are instrumental in putting together proper board packages, they asked me about the backgrounds of each broker. One I knew and I knew that she would deliver a perfect application, even though hers was the lower bid. The other broker I had never met before and I had no information to vouch for his board application acumen. Given the potential buyers had similar financial profiles, the seller went with broker number one and the lower price, stating he couldn't take a chance the sale not going through due to the board rejecting the sale.

Divorce is one of those emotional events that can easily turn sellers into desperate sellers, so anxious are they to be rid of the other person. If the proceeds are to be divided, it is not below the party still in residence or who has the most control to either resist the sale as long as possible, or to accept the lowest offer, so their former spouse gets less money.

In a heated market, when prices are climbing, owners are encouraged to list their homes at inflated prices, just in case someone with millions of dollars might pay it. Mostly these are sellers who are testing the market. The words that make us want to run in the other direction are, "We're not in a hurry." No doubt we have seen buyers willing to pay the extra price because they believe the numbers will continue to go up. As of this writing, these listings are gathering a bit more dust these days, and smart sellers are listening to their expert brokers and dropping their astronomical prices.

In a changing market, don't inch down. Jump ahead of the competition, by pricing lower than the comparable homes, and you might just grab that one buyer who has to buy and sees the price reduction as an opportunity. One of my favorite quotes is from Baron Rothschild. When asked how he made so much money in the stock market, he said, "I never buy at the bottom and I always sell too soon."

The seller who knows it is best to trust an expert is a smart seller and is willing to hear the truth in numbers and market conditions. They know how to rely on those in the field. I have found that they are most often leaders in their own industries, know how to delegate, and allow those who report to them to do their job. A willing seller is a winning seller, and we have seen the universe line up to reward them. The market is always in their favor. They also reward those who help them achieve the results they desire. In other words, they are return customers and believe in buying and selling with the same broker. It builds strength and loyalty, and strengthens the buyer's or seller's own team of experts, whom they can work with again and again.

We were recently the second broker on a listing that had been overpriced. We didn't know the owner, had been referred to him through someone who lived in his building and with whom we had done business. The apartment, while beautifully renovated, was overfilled with furniture. The first thing we suggested was that he allow us to go in and do some serious staging. The owner trusted us. He also agreed to our pricing and to take the apartment off the market for a few weeks while we prepared it. We spent a day rearranging, including changing the use of one room from a library to a dining room, which was an easy fix for a seven-room home that appeared not to have a place to eat. Most of the other changes were to remove some furnishings and open up spaces to allow the sense of air, light, and space. For instance, there was a table that blocked access to the living room windows. It had two large lamps with equally large shades. Flanking the table were two high-backed chairs. Not only did it hinder access to windows, but you also had to walk sideways to get around the chair legs and into the next room. These obstacles give buyers a sense that there is a lack of space, so we removed it all, and suddenly the room breathed. We would arrive early for appointments to show the home, to open the drapes and shades to the lovely sunlight and views.

We brought in our professional photographer and the apartment shined, in person and in our photos, and the owner's eclectic combination of antique furniture and cutting-edge modern art collection created a stunning juxtaposition in the pristine prewar home.

We had immediate interest and sold the apartment very quickly. The only complaint from the owner was that he couldn't find the alarm clock that we had tucked under the bed for the photo shoot.

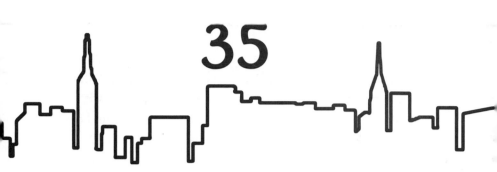

35

Table 43: Dinner With the Rennas

Alfred, Donna, and I had just been seated at our favorite table at the Regency, which we'd booked with a maître d' whom we'd known for years. We were back in the city from an off-season weekend out on the island. "Out on the island" to a New Yorker means that you have traveled to Long Island. It usually implies the Hamptons, unless you are visiting the town you grew up in, which is likely to have been up island. If you are a local heading up island, it usually means heading west to a mid-island mall. There is even a mall once called the Mid-Island Shopping Plaza (now the Broadway Mall).

Our table, coveted dining real estate, was one of three cozy banquettes up a step from the main dining floor and from where one could look out over all of the rich and famous. Just as we had settled in and ordered drinks, we heard a voice from the direction of the bar.

"Hi, guys. We haven't all been together since Club 18!" Club 18 was what we used to call the eighteenth floor at Corcoran when Alfred was the sales manager. Donna and I had shared a corner office with Linda, who had just arrived to have a reunion dinner with us. In those days, Alfred's office was right next door, and we could hear his entire day's goings-on. The best part was the end of the day, when everyone just hung out. We would spill out into the hallway, laughter filling every evening. The overflow of people would end up in our office. We all loved Club 18. Alfred had handpicked every person who got a desk on that floor. Then the day came when Douglas Elliman came calling with a better deal, a bigger office, more money, and more power, and the fun ended when Alfred went off to the enemy. It was real estate mutiny and lots of brokers jumped ship and followed. Every day another desk was vacated. Sad good-bye emails followed. Every day, brokers came by our office saying, "Is it time to pack our bags and head down the street?"

"I miss the Rennas," Linda said. "It is so good to see you guys. What are you drinking?"

"Alfred and I are having Chopin martinis with fresh orange," I replied.

"I'm having wine." Donna piped in.

"Hmm." Linda considered. "I'll have the 'tini."

It didn't take much alcohol to loosen all of our tongues concerning who had what, who did what, who said what, and who got what. After all, we were not just there for the love; we all had lots to barter. "So did you hear who got 999?" As in 999 Fifth Avenue, but the numbers have been changed to protect the innocent.

"I heard."

"I heard."

"We all heard."

"Linda, you lived there and knew the owner before it was converted from a rental building to a condo. Why didn't you get it?"

"I don't know. I cried that I didn't, but to tell you the truth, I didn't sell anything there." Linda grew up at 999, eventually giving up the rent-stabilized apartment that she had taken over from her parents but staying in the building, having negotiated a long lease closer to market rate. Then when the owner decided to convert the building, he bought her out of her lease.

"Let's face it. Those apartments are a hodgepodge," Donna said with sympathy—had Linda gotten the exclusive to sell the units in the building, we would have praised its fabulous layouts and gorgeous kitchens instead. As we wrapped up our conversation, and tables in the restaurant emptied, Alfred asked for the bill.

"Dinner is on me, well, actually Elliman."

A few weeks later, Alfred called, speaking in a low, secretive tone. "Have I got news for you."

"Who's leaving?" I said in a low conspirator's tone as well. In our world, "news" means someone is making a move. In fact, in many a corporate world, it is the same. I turned to my assistant and said, "Lenny, close the door."

"Linda."

"Linda?"

"Linda."

"So that's why you said dinner was on Elliman."

"Maybe." This was a shocker. Everyone knew Linda was a *favorite*. Okay, so *favorite* in real estate terms means, *one that is fed* or a broker who is given prime leads for listings and buyers by the company. Offering to give good brokers business is big business. "Don't say anything. She's on her way now."

Linda, one of the top brokers at Corcoran, immediately expanded her success at Elliman. They sure had something special going on over there!

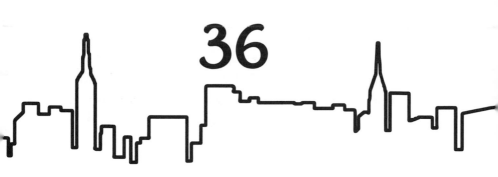

36

The Rise of Broker Assistants

L enny, who has been my assistant for eighteen years, is the ultimate people person, making friends, sharing food and recipes, and offering plans with other brokers, and other broker assistants. He befriends the office staff, who never seem to tire of showing him how to navigate computer functions when need be. He schmoozes with doormen, building managers, managing agents, attorneys, and everyone in between. When important papers are not to be found or we need some inside information, Lenny has no qualms about calling in favors. This unique skill has been a great help, especially after we made the move to Douglas Elliman and many of our files were missing. The most important documents were replaced after Lenny made a few calls. The time we had a board change their decision, it was Lenny who went over to the building for tête-à-tête with the super. In their clandestine meeting, Lenny learned that the sale price was too low for the board's taste and he learned exactly how much would make the deal more palatable.

The most important skill an assistant should have is organizational skills. Lenny, despite his intelligence and charm, is not always organized. If you stop by our office, the desk with multiple shopping bags underneath and various piles in disarray would be Lenny's. Somehow, he always finds what we need, often along with a glove or a muffin he has misplaced. Since no one actually retires from real estate, there are no age limitations, no thresholds to cross, except maybe a Florida condo, New York City brokers keep on selling, and I expect all of us will be negotiating deals for a long time.

Alfred and I have begun to notice that some of the newer broker assistants these days behave as though they are equally as important as the brokers they assist. They know how to get things done, displaying a perfect sense of confidence with a good dose of snobbery, and if they are smart and well educated, it is a very potent combination. Some are so good at their jobs working for top brokers that they earn more money than the average brokers who prefer to work on their own.

It's tough to find and keep a long relationship with a great assistant. A broker must evaluate the cost of time in training someone to be an extension of themselves, which can easily take a year or more, before the assistant is able to predetermine your needs and be in sync with you. Their positions require incredible dexterity, especially when the market is booming. One moment they are setting up appointments for you to take a new buyer on a tour of homes, and the next they are juggling showings at various exclusive listings spread all over town. In between, they are the liaison between you and all of the company's departments, and there are always requirements for all sorts of forms. Then there are the onerous board applications. You must have someone willing to put in long hours, check emails continuously, and be available at all times for showing apartments and conducting open houses. The more they do, the more time we brokers have to be rain-makers. Our most important job is to bring in business and go on appointments, whether to obtain new potential business or consummate business. Lenny is brilliant at setting up appointments, which is crucial for brokers to get their listings. The bottom line is, if you don't show you don't sell, and selling is the ultimate goal.

Alfred was telling me about one of his brokers who asked him to interview a potential broker's assistant.

"Let me tell you about this woman who came to my office for an interview!" he started out. "It's a story, Joanne." A friend of the broker recommended the woman to him. She had come in wearing a low-cut black dress and big heels, and had big hair. It was apparent she was not comfortable being interviewed in a business environment.

"Well, her body language was, shall we say, not quite like one looking to assist in real estate. I would have hired her on the spot had I been a film director. She looked like a brunette Bridgette Bardot with a tattoo of a cobra around her ankle." He had tried to make her feel comfortable. Unfortunately, she was unable to answer any of the questions he asked. "So I babbled for ten minutes about real estate to get to the point where I could wind it up and not have her feel embarrassed." Quickly thereafter, he called up the broker who had been hoping to add her to his team, and asked him to come to his office. The broker walked in anxiously, asking Alfred if he thought she could help him grow his business.

"No doubt various film stars could segue into fantastic brokers assistants," Alfred told his broker as he googled her and found she had some interesting film credits to her name, "but I'm not sure that working in a real estate office is the right fit for her." As brokers come from many careers and backgrounds, so do our highly valued assistants.

A great right-hand person to hire is the privileged trust-funder still fresh from wearing their private-school blazer. I should mention, broker assistants are paid on salary, and if the broker is picking up the tab, that includes paying social security taxes and all sorts of other fees. The trust-funder who might not have figured out what they want to do with their life could make an excellent assistant because he or she often comes to the business by way of their parents. Why not a position in a real estate company? Hiring the trust-funder as a junior broker instead of an assistant is perfect if you don't want to pay a salary, as they don't need the money and are happy to say they have a desk in an office. But do put them to work showing apartments—they look good; have good people skills; are well-spoken, well mannered, well-read, well-traveled; and belong to the best clubs. They allow high-end customers to feel at ease and taken care of. Just beware, they are in Palm Beach or Aspen at all appropriate holidays and long weekends, leaving the broker with a list of things to do.

The spinster assistants are surprisingly not as common as they are in other industries—it must be the money. If a broker is willing to pay a little more, they will get someone fiercely loyal, who will never give up any information about their business and never need to take days off for sick children, because they don't have any, though they could have a feline companion needing a vet visit. They willingly take care of not only your real estate business, but also feel it is an honor when you ask them to handle your personal business as well. They want to be indispensable to you and possibly even be in your will. It's worth letting them learn that you have, in fact, taken care of their future should they outlive you.

These days, we have college graduates who are unable to find jobs. Clearly they are overqualified for the job of assistant, but what you gain is their knowledge of technology, their ability to do Excel spreadsheets and analysis for your investor customers, and the ability to set you up on social media and handle all of the traffic. They troubleshoot any challenge you have on your smartphone and seamlessly get you set up on the newest version as they come available.

They will willingly pick up a daily latte for you, especially if you are treating them to theirs, and they will start bringing in rental business as their college friends are in need of shared apartments.

The next category of those team members who make our hectic lives run smoother are the drivers. I don't have just a driver; I have a saint, a bodyguard, and, most important, a friend and confidant.

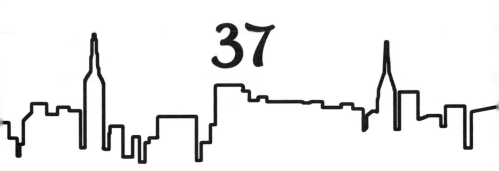

37

Secret Agent Man

"Oh, you know I would follow you anywhere." Ed often begins his sentences with "Oh" in his lilting French accent. He is the tall, handsome man in the driver's seat of my car. On various occasions, he is mistaken for Morgan Freeman. I've watched people's heads spin around. A few have asked him for his autograph. Never mind that I'm the one he's just opened the back door of the car for. But this we only do on certain occasions; we call it the full monty.

"Ed, in all reality, I've been following you around all these years." We both laughed. We have been together for fifteen years. Ed is very imposing and impeccably dressed. In fact, he's got more coordinated outfits than I do, from perfectly crisp shirts and suits, to his silk pocket squares.

One time, when we were running around town in a Range Rover, Ed was taking Donna and me to Sant Ambroeus up on Madison Avenue for a quick espresso break. As we eased into a prime double parking spot, three black SUVs pulled up alongside, blocking us in with their triple parking.

"Ed, check this out." Secret Service agents jumped out of all three cars, suit jackets flapping, revealing firearms.

"Let's do the full monty, Ed!" Donna said as she did a fast red-lipstick check in the mirror and Ed slipped his mirrored sunglasses from his pocket. He stepped out of the car and looked around, holding his jacket closed with one hand and adjusting his Bluetooth with the other as he moved around the car, watching for potential assassins, before opening the doors for us. The real Secret Service were thrown into a tizzy.

Who are they? Thought we had three cars? I imagined them saying into their lapels. Multiple heads jerked around as we each alighted from the car, donning our own mirrored Ray-Bans. Ed sprinted to Sant Ambroeus's door and opened it for us after a quick look to ascertain that the coast was clear. We raced in and claimed our spots at the coffee bar, all eyes looking in our direction, the conversational din barely dimmed but never ceasing. Several of the men in black cautiously followed us and attempted to inconspicuously do a premise check. We stole the initial bit of interest and maybe the thrill one might experience with the possibility of being in the presence of a famous person, but as we're not so famous, by the time whoever needed so much protection came in, everyone was back to concentrating on their own chatter and cappuccinos.

Ed drives expertly, melting through traffic jams and always getting me to my appointments on time. He also doubles as a bodyguard. He has been known to ask me and my clients to wait in the car so that he can check out a building before we go in. It's a special sense he has about possible danger. On one trip to a ragged strip of buildings out in Brooklyn, where a customer and I were invited to an artist's loft, Ed locked us in the car and disappeared for a few minutes. Not only had he checked the building's entry, but also the stairwells. He learned from the guard on duty the day prior that there had been a murder in the elevator, which was still shut down and sealed with police tape. We hiked up several flights with Ed waiting till he heard the artist welcome us into her space and quickly secure it with a commercial-sized bolt on her door.

Ed knows all kinds of people all over town, not to mention multitudes of doormen and other drivers from whom he ascertains all sorts of interesting secrets. It is not uncommon for someone to pull up beside us and, next thing you know, windows are open and rapid conversation crosses lanes before the light changes. Then, should there be a need of any sort, Ed has a friend. One weekend when I was out east, driving myself, a deer shot across Main Street, hitting the corner of my car. When Ed took it to the dealership back in the city, the estimate for the repair, which entailed replacing a corner piece of plastic, was $3,000. Ed called me and said he had left and was heading to Queens, where he had a friend. His friend ordered the part from Range Rover for $150 and replaced it with touch-ups for another $150. Total repair: $300. Cash only.

Another day, I had a family of three in the backseat who had flown into town for just two days to find an apartment. Lenny had set up back-to-back appointments, but on day one, the skies turned black and there was a soaking rain. One umbrella was not going to keep us all dry. Ed pulled up to the Regency Hotel and hopped out. He was back in a moment with a huge hotel umbrella, courtesy of a friend who worked there as a concierge. I finally asked him how he managed to know so many people. It turned out, he is a member of the Freemasons. Through certain subtle hand and head signals that only another member would know, and which they acknowledge with another signal, they recognize each other.

It's kind of like magic, first how someone just happens to be where you are and then has just what you need.

Through Ed, I feel a certain sense of security, as if there are guardian angels all over town.

Ed and I have been through life's extremes together. He was with me beside Jonathan's bed when Jonathan took his last breaths. I was in the car with Ed when he learned that his daughter and son-in-law were assassinated in Haiti. Both had been receiving death threats, she for her work with Doctors Without Borders and he for being the head of the largest human rights organization in Haiti. It wasn't until that day that I learned of the work they did. It seems Ed and his extended family focus much of their lives on giving and helping others, yet seldom does he even mention it. Ed and I have grieved with and for each other, and we have rejoiced as well—all the while circling Manhattan.

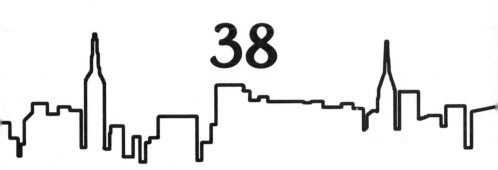

38

Negotiating Seats

It was late 2014, and Alfred, Paul, and I had been planning a trip
to Italy for a few months that coincided with a destination wedding Alfred had been invited to. The son of one of his brokers and
Elliman's very talented marketing young lady were tying the knot
in Taormina, Italy, and their friends and family were flying in from
all corners of the world. The nuptials were four weeks away, and the
previous weekend, we had spent hours on the computer checking
airfares and hotels, and calling American Express. They must have
the slowest computers in the world just so they can say, "While we're
waiting for this to come up..." and tell you about all sorts of stuff
you've heard about already, but you simply can't stop them. I think
they get bonus points for the number of words they spit out per minute. Come to think of it, they'd make great New York City brokers.

So, day one, two calls to AMEX, several online searches, and hours later, we still had no reservations. Well, I don't know if it comes with the territory in searching out the best, but we just knew we could get first-class tickets for less than $16,000 for the three of us.

Back in the city just a day later, and bingo, another search and Alitalia came up with round-trip tickets for all of us for $8,400. Alfred and I discussed the options by phone while I grabbed lunch.

"Why don't I come to Elliman?" I suggested

"Sure. What are you doing now?"

"Standing at the coffee bar at Sant Ambroeus, having a panini and a cappuccino."

"So come over now." I waved my AMEX Platinum to get the barista's attention. "I need to run," I mouthed. Without asking, he grabbed my coffee, poured it into a take-out cup, and I was out the door, my panini in hand just as Ed was pulling up in front. "Ed, I'm going to Douglas Elliman."

On my way, Alfred put me on speakerphone on his cell, while he dialed AMEX from his office phone. "Oh, that's sounds awfully cheap," the very first agent chirped. I could hear Alfred tearing his hair out.

"Alfred! ALFRED!" I stage-whispered. "She doesn't know what she's talking about." I took the last bite of my panini and said, "Hang up. I'm almost there."

"I did. She had me on hold. Joanne, Sandy has invited you and Paul to the wedding, for the third time. I think she really wants you to go."

"I feel funny. I don't really know them," I said.

"It's Italy," Alfred said, sounding exasperated. "Everyone goes to the wedding."

"Okay, we'll go."

"Where are you now?"

"Just pulling up to 575." I hopped out with my six-dollar coffee. Isn't that insane? It didn't even include a stool at the counter; it's standing only, just like in Italy. Throw in a panini or two if you're a bit hungry, and you're over twenty bucks. "It's all about the real estate," Lorenzo, one of our favorite maître d's, once said as he spread his hands out like a saint over the pink marble café counter.

When I got to the fifth floor, Alfred had the Alitalia website up. "Oy," he said, leaning precariously over the arm of his chair.

"Is your back bothering you?"

"My kinesiologist said it's emotional stress."

"Maybe you need therapy—real estate therapy."

Just then, a blondish broker walked into Alfred's office without knocking. "I wanted to see your sister!" she exclaimed.

"Oh, hi . . . " I said, hesitant.

"Hi!" She gave me a weak handshake. "You don't remember me!"

I thought, *Do we all talk in explanation points? Is it a side effect of our business?* "Didn't we do something together?" I asked, trying to recall what and from where—a sale? A rental? Maybe Lenny had shown her one of our listings?

"No, but you showed my three-bedroom exclusive at 120 East Sixty-Sixth!" I wracked my brain. "The one with the stunning kitchen, and black granite counters and floors," she reminded me.

"Oh! That's it!" I exclaimed. "How are you?"

"Great! I just love your brother." Broker formalities done, she launched into her spiel. "I wouldn't mind both of your input."

"Consider it group therapy," Alfred said. She set the scene of her potential deal, and we hashed out various offers, possible responses, and pros and cons of the property: great views but low ceilings; how many days it had been on the market (over three hundred, but the price was just lowered); what the monthly charges were ($12,500); why it hadn't sold; and that it was not a family-friendly building.

I won't say who said that because it's not legal for us to say those things, even if they might be true.

We should mention that larger people, as long as they can walk, are not on the protected list of persons that co-op boards are not allowed to discriminate against. I mention this only because I know someone in the business who bumped into the president of his board the morning after a very nice and very wealthy couple had their interview. Mind you, the building required one have three times the purchase price in liquid assets *after* the purchase of the multimillion-dollar home. The president told him he just couldn't imagine riding the elevator with "such a big woman" and that he had voted to turn the couple down. The elevator in the building was unusually small, despite the fact that most of the apartments had twelve rooms each—I still wonder how that board president gets his big ego into it.

Back to massaging the deal: we all came to the same starting number—not too low but certainly not near the asking price because we all know that a postwar building with low ceilings on Park Avenue is not really a proper Park Avenue building. And the broker got up to leave.

"Thank you so much, you guys!"

Alfred pressed redial while I closed the door.

"Thank you for calling American Express. Please say or press your card number."

"We are looking for the best-priced seats to Italy, first or business class only, fully reclining seats. We'll change dates and airports if necessary but don't bother looking around: go right to Alitalia. They have tickets for $2,811 round-trip per person." A moment's pause. "We know all about that . . . Yes, we know all about that too. We've already done that . . . Yes, we know it's Labor Day." We were finally booked for our flight and even the flight down to Sicily for the Sicilian-style wedding. The next day, we would search for hotels, scrutinizing every website, photo, map, and satellite shot to find the best price for the best five-star property in the best location.

"Alfred, we could all share a room," I joked.

"No way!" It was looking like a very interesting trip.

Three weeks later, we were boarding our flight.

We were examining our flatbed seats with personal entertainment panels while flight attendants helped stash our carry-on luggage. Our first three nights in Rome were booked in a furnished apartment arranged through our friend Max. We had no other reservations for our fourteen-day excursion through Italy that was to end with the wedding.

We settled into our seats not too sorry we were missing the last lovely day of summer in the Hamptons. We'd be back in time for the crazy October weekends of the pumpkin people, tourists who love the fall foliage and take their kids to pick pumpkins and have fun in the corn mazes of our local farms.

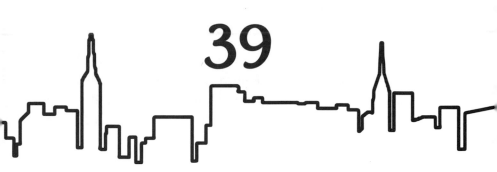

39

Toilet Shopping

In the middle of one of our team meetings, we were interrupted by Donna's cell ringing. "Donna Renna," she barked into her phone. Then, in a flash, her hard-as-nails business voice changed to warm Caribbean sunshine. "Oh, hi, *amore*." Next, we heard murmuring and then, "So Daniela has to drive to Chicago to buy a toilet." I could just make out the response through her headset and thought, *Doesn't Daniela live in New Jersey?*

"Because, amore, she will save two hundred fifty dollars."

"Who the heck drives to Chicago for a toilet?" I exclaimed, inserting myself into the conversation.

Michael, on the other end of the line, had a similar response: "What the heck is wrong with Home Depot?"

As we are all building and renovating all the time, discussing toilet choices has been part of our group counsel before. The latest dialogue has entailed whether to go floor mount or the newer, easy-to-clean-under wall mount. Wall-mount toilets are like sculpture for the bathroom, and they float over your tile or stone, while the flushing mechanisms glitter above, flat on the wall. They are most often found in nickel or gleaming stainless steel, another design choice Alfred and I were faced with—brushed or glittering. These sleek flushers give you the choice of a half flush or full flush. Another feature of the new toilets are the soft-close lids and seats, which makes you accustomed to giving them a good push. Of course, no one wants to wait for the lid to slowly glide down before the flush, thus the habit to give it a push, which is not a problem till you are a guest in someone's home with old-fashioned toilet seats and you unintentionally slam the lid or both lid and seat.

Coincidently, the weekend following our meeting, we were all out east when Alfred sent a group text asking whoever was available to rush over. "Toilets might have been mounted too low. Can anyone come over ASAP before the plumber gets here?" Rosemary and I jumped in the car and in one minute were at his mid-construction house.

"What should the height be?" Alfred asked. With a floor mount, there's no variable.

"There must be a recommended height," I said. We conferred, checked online, called Donna to see if her friend might have mentioned anything about the toilet she was driving to Chicago for. The problem was Alfred's plumber was not accustomed to wall-mount toilets and had not accounted for how much room would be taken up when the marble floors were installed, making the mounted toilet suddenly quite a bit closer to the floor. We all took turns sitting and compared thoughts on comfort levels till we determined the ideal for most persons.

Prior to having made the final decision on the wall-mount versions, we had gone to several showrooms to look at toilets. Neither Alfred nor I wanted to be in a showroom with brilliant lighting that makes all the bathroom stuff look even shinier and sit on a toilet or figure out which way to straddle a bidet. I've never seen anyone else give them trial runs and wonder how everyone makes their decisions. Over at Home Depot, the toilets are hung on a wall about eight feet high, I suspect so no one uses them. One salesman at one of the fancy showrooms we were visiting told us they had discovered a for-display-only toilet had been used. At yet another showroom, the saleswoman saw us eyeing a toilet and rushed over to encourage us to visit a nearby New York City restaurant, where the very clever manufacturer had installed, for free, their latest seat-warming toilet with built-in booty sprayer, suggesting that we might enjoy giving it try along with the excellent sushi there.

While we were hanging around Alfred's master bathroom waiting for the plumber, Alfred on the rim of the toilet, Rosemary on the rim of bidet, and me on the rim of the tub, we recounted toilet stories. I told them about an older friend who was the widow of a movie mogul and who might be called the queen of the throne. Tessie was born brunette, poor, and with a rather large nose. As soon as she saved up enough money working as a seamstress, she had a nose job, bleached her hair blond, and changed her Bronx accent to that of a New York socialite. It wasn't long before she married well. Tessie is lovely and enchanting, yet she speaks of nothing that has any depth.

The summer of 2014, she was approached to sell her town house and invited all of her friends to a last summer soiree. The French doors were opened, and a wonderful breeze blew through. Tessie sat on a little stool in the middle of the living room, not a blond hair moving, and her guests towering over her. She proceeded to discourse at great length about toilet paper and a friend of hers, not present, who did not know how to properly purchase or hang toilet paper with the end coming over the top of the roll. She lectured on the correct softness, how to fold the edges just before leaving the seat, the pros and cons of scented paper, and how it is best used, folded not scrunched or vice versa, depending. Then she moved on to proper toilet etiquette and how one should "hold back a bit" if you are a guest, especially if the powder room is in earshot of other guests. She had everyone's rapt attention. I was not alone when I decided not to finish my drink and hold it in till I got home.

When Alfred first started in the business, he had a buyer whose priority was the positioning of the toilet. The oversized gentleman's criteria included fitting on the throne and whether or not he could get back up easily. Every apartment Alfred showed, the buyer headed straight to the bathroom. "If the seat was up," Alfred said, "he'd drop it down, and there was no soft close in those days. Then he'd back up into the seat, like this." As he demonstrated, I asked him if his buyer ever got stuck. "I had to help him once. He got stuck between the vanity and the wall, and I had to pull him out. He did eventually buy a very nice garden apartment in Queens and all the bathroom fixtures were the formerly popular color known as harvest gold."

The lengths we all go to for the betterment of our abodes and bodies. One person's quest may be for the best deal on a seat-warming toilet. Alfred has been hunting down an affordable Italian midcentury sofa; mine is for the most sublime lighting fixtures that whisper their presence, sing their design brilliance, and make us all glow and look years younger. Others search till they find the perfect toilet experience, and there are so many choices of upgrades, much like buying a new car. Donna's friend was getting ready to drive 778.9 miles for her dream toilet, and just the week before, I was showing a couple and their two young adult children apartments in a new building where the bathrooms were top of the line. The toilets had lids that automatically rose as you entered the bathroom and closed as you exited. As we took turns moving in and out of the bathrooms during the tour, the lids were going up and down, up and down, while the listing broker expounded on all of its other functions with a straight face. I had to suck in my cheeks not to break out laughing.

When Donna hung up with Michael, she called their friend back to suggest that she might find the perfect toilet right there in Jersey.

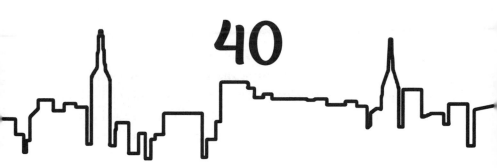

40

At the Coffee Bar

Our favorite café has a location in the Hamptons, and we have been going for years, since Francesca and her husband opened up for business.

"Alfred, how long have I been telling you, you have to stop by and see Francesca?"

"I don't know. Four months?"

"Let's not forget that time we all went Downtown to have a downtown kind of brunch."

"Oh, yeah, and every single place had a wait time of two hours."

"It was unreal . . . so remember what we did, Joanne?"

"Yes, Donna called the West Village Sant Ambroeus Café and we made a reservation, jumped in a cab, and were sitting down to ricotta pancakes in less time than it takes to check your coat at Spice Market."

"That's right."

"And that's why I got nervous you weren't going for coffee and to see Francesca when I was sure she knew you had been out in Southampton every weekend. Whenever she saw Paul and me there, she'd ask where you were. Finally, I told her about the bad barista."

"You have no idea how bad he was—and rude too. He was very rude to me."

"He was rude to everybody. I told you they let him go after two weeks."

"But the signora should have said something. But okay. We went back in."

We did, on a cold Saturday afternoon. So there we were, at the end of the coffee bar. Signora was down by the register. The holidays had finally ended. She and I caught each other's eye and she mouthed *Happy New Year* in Italian, but clearly not to Alfred.

Felice anno nuovo, I mouthed back.

She cut a side glance at Alfred, looked back, and turned her nose up at him with a finger wagging that clearly said, *Non felice anno nuovo a Alfredo*.

"She's angry at me."

"I told you she was angry at you."

"She's not coming down here, is she?"

"No, she's not coming down here." He tilted his cup to sip every drop of what might be his last cappuccino in that café and glared back down to the other end of the long marble counter at the signora, arms folded across her chest, pearls heaving and glinting in the winter sun. I'm telling you, Francesca and Alfred were two cowboys in an old spaghetti western, waiting to see who would draw first. Mind you, this café is a very Northern Italian establishment, and the proprietors are a good-looking older couple; she still classically beautiful, like what Grace Kelly might have looked like now, he, white hair, mustache, wire-rimmed glasses, perfectly tailored tweed jackets. They look like an ad for something very expensive and very Swiss, like Patek Philippe watches.

"You might need this." *Signore*, signora's husband, came over with a very pointy, serrated knife.

What the heck do they cut with that? I thought.

He solemnly laid it on the counter in front of Alfred.

"I'm going to have to go talk to her," Alfred said solemnly.

"Yes," the signore and I answered with equal gravitas.

"Yes."

"Alfred. Come on . . . let's go pay," I said.

Alfred reached over the counter to grab our bill. He left the knife untouched. His eyes were squinted. Signore slowly slipped the knife out of sight, shrugging as if to say, *I tried.* We all headed to the register on our respective sides of the bar.

"Alfred," I whispered as we made our way. "We'll have to sell our houses if you don't get this feud settled!" We love our town not just for the sandy beach, but also for our café. "And tell her about your surgery."

"Signora."

"Alfredo."

"I've never won, not one time," signore said, standing at a safe distance. Then, not a sound, not even from some of the other customers, who were stopping in their tracks, cups in midair, lips mid words, bills clutched in hands. All eyes were on us.

No one even breathed, till finally Signora spit out, "You should have come to *me!*"

"What do you mean, come to you?"

"You complained to my son."

"What? I never complained to your son."

"We fired that man after two weeks, and you don't come here for months."

"I had surgery!"

"So, so, you had surgery. So what? Did you die? You couldn't call me? You couldn't come in?"

"I didn't, but neither did I say a word to your son."

"No?"

"I would never have complained to anyone but you. Look. You've known me now for what? Twenty years? Since you opened, I've been coming here."

They spewed who did what, said what, dueling till the flames began to burn out.

I broke out into a cold sweat.

"So what was wrong with you?" she asked.

Thank you, God, I thought. *We are close to a truce.* Alfred went on to give her the details of his symptoms and his surgery. He pulled down his shirt and showed her the two-inch scar at the base of his neck. Then she held out two fingers, crossing them back and forth over each other.

"Okay, so maybe I put two and two together. I thought it was you who complained."

"Will you two please shake hands and make up?" I said. They looked at me for a moment as they considered.

Then as they reached over the cash register she said warmly, "Are you okay now?"

There was a collective sigh of relief. You'd almost have expected there to be applause. Then signora turned to me and said, "And so, where has your sister Rosemary been? She doesn't come in to see me before she moves!"

This is why we love our café, at the beach and in the city—Uptown, Midtown, and Downtown. It's a slice of Italy, the old ways of honor, kissing the ring, knowing the value of the few inches of stone counter you lease when you happily pay for the best cappuccino this side of the Atlantic. It is a place of history, like the squares, gates, and marketplaces of ancient crossroads, a place of good old-fashioned bartering in gossip. It is where overlapping tribe members meet. You never know whose elbow you might be bumping. The voices of many nations chatter, people kiss-kiss in the air, handshakes seal deals and new alliances. It is the ultimate in New Yorkers negotiating without technology, just a cup of coffee.

The Gatekeepers

New York has all sorts of gatekeepers. The most visible are our doormen and concierges, which in some buildings are separate positions and in other buildings the same, and they come in all types. For instance, we've got what we like to refer to as the *CIA Doormen*. They love working in Trump buildings, where they get to wear a discreet kind of earpiece. These men and women are always dressed in well-tailored dark suits—very CIA or even Secret Service like. You can imagine them trotting alongside the presidential motorcade. As a broker, you must have the equivalent of high-security clearance, just short of a pat down, to be able to get in and show your listing. And they always remember your name. "That's because I think they are accustomed to memorizing dossiers, faces, and aliases," Alfred likes to say.

Another familiar doorman personality is the kibitzer. They chew
your ear off on the way in and on the way out. If you've got one in
your own building, you wait until they are distracted putting away
a UPS delivery, and then you make a dash for the door. These doormen are the first to know whose husband or wife is cheating, and
their stock in trade in lobby life is rumors and scandals. They watch,
listen, and ask just the right questions from each party passing in and
out the door, spreading their questions over all participating tenants. By the end of the day, they've got the full scoop, including who
the divorce attorney will be and how much money has been hidden. You can spot them by their posture—leaning on their podium,
ear turned to whomever is speaking in confessional whispers. If it's
really hot information, they won't even notice you prying open the
door with your foot, your arms full of shopping bags.

The aloof doorman takes ownership of their building and looks
down their nose at you should you deign to enter. They could make
even a member of the Daughters of the American Revolution feel
like they just got off the boat. His close cousin is the border patrol
doorman, who may make you show your papers just to get to your
apartment. If you are not recognized by one of these gentlemen,
they take an inordinate amount of time to think and survey your
demeanor before disturbing one of their precious tenants, even if it's
your godmother.

Our doormen and concierges contribute to New York life in all
sorts of ways. Their information network extends beyond building and neighborhood gossip and includes pertinent information
regarding the sale of apartments. These lines of communication
are handled in the time-honored way of passing information from
doorman to doorman, from one building to another. One doorman
tells his comrade across the street. That doorman tells another in
the building next door, that one to the one around the corner. It's
mouth to ear, and they like it this way. Before you know it, a door-

man working in a building blocks away will know if a buyer did not pass muster with a board. Don't even think about lying on the next board application that asks if you have ever been turned down by a board, because word will have gotten to the next building you attempt to purchase in. That happened to customers of mine. Before I met them, the board in a certain upscale white-brick building had turned them down. I knew exactly why and assured them I would get them board approval at the next building they applied to. A perfect classic six-room apartment came up ten blocks away, this time in a redbrick building. I showed it. They loved it. I called the owner with their offer, and financial and employment background. When she got back to me with a counteroffer, she had already ascertained, through the doorman network, that this lovely couple had failed to pass in the cooperative they'd applied to before. The owner was infuriated to hear that it was likely due to their religious background and immediately contacted the board president of her building to lay the groundwork for board approval.

They passed with flying colors on their next purchase—and this time it was in a better building and in a superior location.

Another doorman side service is fashion approval. Alfred has real pressure in his building. "My lobby is like a fashion runway. Our concierge lets you know whether or not he approves of your outfit and curls his lip up with disdain when you haven't quite pulled it all together." When Alfred knows he's not hitting the mark, he waits for the concierge to be distracted with a package before darting out the door. "There are so many details I have to consider: Did I accessorize properly, with the right watch? Does the color of my necktie pick up a color in my suit? Are my shoes perfectly buffed? Is every hair in place? It's a lot of pressure."

I feel the same though my building is more on the casual side. My doorman will notice if I'm in gym gear and say, "Off to the gym? Good for you!" I always feel like I get extra points when my super sees me in my gym clothes because he's always working out and is packed with muscle. It's a lot of pressure to dress right for the gym and keep my stomach sucked in.

Another very important person in our line of work is the building superintendent, who we like to refer to as *il capo di co-op* or *il capo di condo*, as the case may be. These days they are now called building managers. They all have a cousin who is a superintendent in another building. These positions are sacred and coveted, and getting in is like getting into a club or becoming a Freemason. Supers get to live in the building they are managing, so the more prestigious the address, the more prestigious their position. Building managers are the king of their domain, and one must learn the art of negotiating with them whether a tenant looking for a leaky faucet to be fixed, a broker looking to sell, a buyer looking to buy, an architect looking to design an apartment, or a contractor looking to renovate, all will need access to information only the super will have. There is a culture of *superdom*. Their office is in the basement and decorated with discarded antiques, artificial flowers, and donated artwork painted by the little darlings of the tenants. For others of such exalted posts, there is a handsomely appointed, windowed office off the lobby.

The parking garage managers are also very important gatekeepers, and even in this age, most are still men, including the superintendents or building managers. The parking garage managers are like the pope of a building. They have more power than the entity that actually owns the garage. If you want a spot, you talk to the manager. If you want a special spot, you talk to the manager. If you have an extra fancy car, you better talk to the manager. In fact, unless you are parking a car worth less than your monthly payment for the privilege of parking, when you talk to the manager, you need to have dollar signs falling out your mouth and your pocket. My parking garage manager is the best. I want to take him and turn him into a super broker. He is cute, has an amazing personality, is happily married, and is the cheeriest brand-new father I ever met.

I once commented to Alfred, "In three years I haven't had one ding in my car. He puts Ed's car in my spot—"

"The key there is you *have* a personal spot."

"Yes, so I don't have to call an hour ahead of time because a dozen other cars need to be moved first. He cleans the car, helps me with my luggage, offers to walk or drive me to the apartment, and is the best in the whole city.

I heard about a fascinating New York City parking garage ritual concerning getting your car out when you need it. The husband of one of my book club members said they had to give an exact time they would pick up their cars in the morning. They both commute to New Jersey, where they used to live. By exact time, you have say that you will be in your car, ready to pull out at 7:21 AM or 7:23 AM, and so on. All the cars going out are lined up on the ramp in order, as each owner requires. You must be sitting in your car ready to pull out at your appointed time. If you miss your time, everyone is late and you lose your morning spot. It all sounded like way too much pressure. It reminded me of another ritual, the mani/pedi, and a nail salon I used to go to where there was a rigid schedule one had to keep and one tough gatekeeper.

I learned about the salon through a customer who was a well-known and beautiful dermatologist. Her nails were always perfect, and she recommended I might like her nail spa. Believe it or not, I had to have her give me a referral in order to get in. Getting in meant getting a spot on the calendar. There had to be an opening, and it took about three weeks before they called and told me when to arrive. It was to be every third Tuesday at 9:00 AM. I was fascinated at my first visit. My nails were first examined by the Eastern European proprietor. I was given my own set of nail paraphernalia and a cubby to put it in. You dried your nails lounging on the deep, comfortable leather sofas, no hot air machines with UV rays here.

On one of my visits, I watched as the owner strictly trained a new technician on the proper way to file a nail—how to hold the file at a precise angle to the nail, how to move the file in one very careful direction, and so on. It was incredible. But most impressive was the woman manning the door, who would peek through the tiny window to see if the person at the door was a man. NO MEN PERMITTED was the only sign outside indicating it was any sort of establishment. Then she would check her clipboard and watch, make a notation, and buzz you in. One day, I was three minutes late. I had seen what happened to another woman who showed up mere moments past her appointed time. You got one chance. Next time, you lost your spot. Even though it was the best manicure and pedicure I had ever had, and they lasted the full three weeks before my next mandatory appointment, I gave up and went back to my own neighborhood salon.

42

The Cousins

It was ten minutes before our guests were due to arrive. We'd been spending the 2015 holidays at our summer rental property, the North Main house, since Alfred, Paul, and I were still in construction on our own summer homes. Rosemary was with us for the two weeks we were there, and we had invited our favorite Renna cousins, for New Year's Eve, who had followed in their parents' footsteps and also had homes in the Hamptons. Everything was ready with appetizers on the fabulous 1970s glass-and-Plexiglas cocktail table we'd bought from Gina. She had called Alfred earlier that day, and I could hear her booming voice through the phone.

"Ahhhh, we comin' over to your house for drinks? I don't think so!"

"I've been sleeping in that nice bed we paid you an arm and leg for. You using that money for your next flip house?"

Laughter came through the phone.

"Our tenants this summer loved it too. Oh, and I've got my fur-lined-slippered feet up on that coffee table," Alfred said.

I know Gina had had a tinge of regret about the table the first time she came to see our rental property all decorated and photo ready.

"Aghh hahah." Her groan turned into a laugh. "So, how's it goin'? Should I bring champagne . . . not! When is that builder finishing your house already?" Alfred had expected to be in his house by August past.

"Actually, I'm having a fireplace design challenge," Alfred said, avoiding the premise of the question.

"I got a guy. I'll call to pick his brain."

"And I need a front door lock set."

"Go to Simons. I got a girl there, she's a good rep and will get you a deep contractor's discount."

"How's it going on Harvest?" Alfred threw back. While Gina's construction was long completed, from expansion to staging and expecting the same success she'd had on the Burnett House, Harvest was just sitting there, the FOR SALE sign beginning to fade.

"I've got three couples dickin' around. End of the day I got a whole load of nothin'. Plus, we're now living in a house I just bought that has pink brick. I hate it. I immediately put it right back on the market and I got all-cash foreign buyers, made sure the cash was here. So I been runnin' around trying to buy another house before signing the contract."

"Are you still in Manhasset?"

"Nah, Sands Point. So I found another house, and I'm there the other day with the engineer, and I see rat droppings all over the place. The house has rats!"

"Sands Point has rats? I can just imagine you coming down for your morning coffee and hearing them scratching in the walls."

"Yeah. So the engineer says Sands Point has lots of rats but I could get rid of them with a Jack Russell terrier, they're ratters, so I been lookin' around for breeders to get one. Then I say to myself, what do I need another dog for? I got four already, to chase rats in a house I don't even own! So I say to my husband, 'Forget buyin' this house, let's stay where we are till we find somethin' better,' and I gave the deposit money back to the foreign buyer for our house, which I hate."

"So why don't you look for a rental?"

"We were in a rental, paid up front for six months, put up a fence for the dogs; then this ugly house came on the market. There was nothin' else. Bought it, moved again a month later. So now I have this, Harvest, and the house on Hill Street near you, all on the market."

Within the first two minutes of meeting Gina, it was immediate screams, laughing, and fun. We love that Gina buys, fixes, decorates, sells, and does it all again like a junkie. We had hoped she was in Southampton and could join our New Year's Eve soiree. Of course not everyone does things last minute like us. Michael Renna didn't even confirm till two that afternoon even though we invited him the day before, and that was after much cajoling and a promise to have the TV on so he could monitor the football game.

Later that afternoon, we all piled into the car for an antique outing. We are always combing the local shops for great finds. Most recently, we had been focused on great midcentury furniture. We also decided to hit the tile showrooms; then we went as far as Eastport to climb through the moldy antique store that none of us had been to in twenty years. The owners were still sitting just inside the front door, wearing big down coats and had little heaters at their feet. The place was dark, cold, and packed with junk. The husband took us out back to the huge warehouse, also filled to its steel rafters with more junk, absolutely nothing anyone lusts after. There was a FOR SALE sign out front for all four buildings they owned, which made up more than half the town.

"How much are you asking for the property?" I asked.

"One million five hundred. If we get our price, we're getting outta here. Business is dismal. I hate it here." Okay, he didn't say he hated his old town, but it seemed to me their decaying business, which took up nearly half the town in real estate, was contributing to keeping it from progressing to a charming town filled with cafés, galleries, and high-priced decorating stores run by good-looking men with fabulous taste. It was hard to believe that a potentially lovely town on the water looked to be falling to ruin.

Next stop was Riverhead, also for an antique store. I used to love walking through those places on the hunt for some wonderful treasure. Now, I'd rather go to a well-curated shop where someone else has spent hours sniffing out a few gems. We drove back and forth through the town twice. It was a good exercise as I had been researching properties off Main Street, where there are very interesting older homes. Few come on the market. Was this the next frontier for the Hamptons? Riverhead is on the river and sits at the crotch of Long Island's two forks.

"This town is a dump," Alfred said. "I'm done."

"Alfred, there is some very nice architecture here. Look at these buildings." Rosemary said as she put on her glasses to get a better look.

"It's a dump, Rosemary."

"You're right. Too many empty stores, one or two new cafés. Look—there's even a Blue Duck Bakery. I wonder why they opened up here."

"Who cares."

"I figure a few designers will someday buy houses, fix them up, then we'll all want to have houses here." I offered. "Plus it's a good commuting town if you work in the mid-island area.

"The designers are not coming to Riverhead." Alfred countered.

"Maybe." I said. That ended the day's hunt, even for real estate treasure hidden under weeds and plywood. There are so many places where what could have been a charming town in a renaissance that just didn't take. It was time to head back to North Main and get ready for our company and ring in the New Year. We took the scenic route out of Riverhead, past the golf course that sits right on the Peconic Bay (the views are gorgeous), and headed home.

Back at the house, Michael and Paul came in through the back door just as cousins Michele and Tony were ringing a doorbell we didn't know we had, at the front door. The only person who ever came through the front door was Creighton, our irrigation man, and he had a key. Kisses, hugs, and how-are-yous ensued, and we gathered coats to pile on the guest room bed. Drinks were poured, and Michele took a spot on the sofa.

"I'm exhausted. We just moved." She said with a puff.

"You moved?" Rosemary and I said in unison.

"When?" Alfred asked.

"Out here?" My question followed wondering if they were giving up city life.

"No. In the city."

"You mean Brooklyn?" Alfred implying that Brooklyn is not the city. When we say "the city," we still think Manhattan. People from Brooklyn mean Brooklyn first, Manhattan second even though they say they are "going to the city" when coming into Manhattan. It can be confusing.

"From Brooklyn. We moved on December 18. We were going into the city for a matinee, and I've had my eye on a building in the Financial District, right across the street from Tony's office. Apartments rarely come up, and there was an open house, so we went."

"By the intermission," Tony said, picking up, "we'd decided to take the apartment."

"So we called the broker and said we were coming back to sign a lease right after the show," Michele continued.

"So we did."

"Wow, that's fabulous, Michele. Now we'll all be on the same island all year round," Rosemary said, and refilled both of their glasses with Prosecco to toast.

An interesting fact of our lives that most of us don't really think about is that we island hop. We live on Manhattan Island; then we go out to Long Island; then we cross the canal onto the South Fork, to Southampton. Brooklyn is actually a part of Long Island, as is Queens, even though Queens and Brooklyn are thought of as part of the city, outer boroughs of the city, but city nonetheless.

"So what about your house in Brooklyn?" I asked Michele and Tony, but usually Michele is the one who answers.

"I hate that house."

"Aren't you right off Shore Road?" I was imaging that they were quite close to the water, but none of us have ever gotten together as adults outside of Southampton, so we never got to see their Bay Ridge, Brooklyn, home.

"We're two houses off the water. We've got four floors. It's too big, too much work, and I didn't want to deal with two houses anymore."

"You didn't sell it yet, did you?" Alfred asked.

"No we've got twenty years of stuff in it. We took our bed, our dining set, and our clothes."

"So now what?"

"Our neighbor wants to buy it for their kids." Michele and Tony's home is in an old neighborhood where generations of families have stayed rooted and it seems that everyone is connected somehow. When they first met, Tony was a young partner in a law firm, and Michele had come in for an interview. He hired her, and they soon fell in love. Turned out their mothers knew each other for years back in Brooklyn. We spent the rest of the evening eating, drinking, telling stories, and laughing till we couldn't laugh anymore.

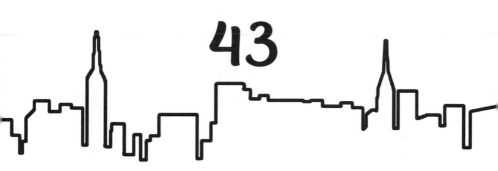

43

Another of Alfred's Craziest Deals: Love's Sad Story

We all enjoy sharing stories of deals, especially those that have unusual or funny situations. One day, Alfred had told me about a couple looking to purchase a love nest in the city. They reminded him of our parents, and how in love they were throughout their marriage.

Mr. and Mrs. Macintosh—upper middle-aged, attractive, sophisticated—were the perfect profile of the empty nesters who kept their season opera tickets at the Met throughout suburban child-raising years and wanted to return to the city. They apparently had the means to purchase before they sold their suburban home and had decided to test drive their new apartment as a *pied-à-terre* to see if it would reignite their passion. This had been clear to their broker by how much the couple would discuss their master suite needs throughout their search, but also, how much they still loved each other.

By the time I met with them, the Macintoshes had a signed contract on a co-op near Lincoln Center, for $2.5 million with $250,000 down in anticipation of their return and active retirement. Their broker had worked on their board package and for five weeks had been requesting supporting documentation of their $45 million net worth, listed on their financial statement under stocks and bonds, and the majority in one stock. The broker had them come to the office so that I, as a manager, could help impress upon them the importance of disclosure and the necessary financial documentation that they had yet to provide. I was concerned that they did not understand that they could have been putting their quarter million dollar down payment in jeopardy.

"There are no statements, we have the actual stock certificates in our bank's vault," the husband said, first looking into his wife's eyes, and then calculating how much stock he'd need to sell to complete the purchase. With his wife bubbling over with love on the side, I couldn't help but think that things at home were already getting stirred up, and they hadn't even closed on their little love nest yet.

I suggested that perhaps they could supplement their stock certificates with an accountant's letter. Mr. M. told me they'd return to Connecticut, meet with their banker, and return the next day with all of the necessary documentation. At this point, they had only shown $3,000 in a checking account.

The next day, Mr. M. called their broker saying he had just remembered that he did not have $45 million in stock but that no one should worry because somehow something would turn up in a few days. The broker became alarmed that her buyer seemed to have no concern, and that he may have sounded confused. She came into my office with a heavy heart and teary-eyed, so together we tracked down one of the couple's sons. He was in shock when we gave him the news that basically we were not able to substantiate there were any liquid assets as his father claimed. The pieces of the puzzle began to fall into place. He filled us in on the incredible tale of how their father surprised his whole family one night at dinner with how much money he had made on one tech stock. He and his sisters had come to think that they had gone from modest middleclass to the heir and heiresses of extraordinary wealth. Their father had told them how he was planning to pay off all of their bills and that he was going to purchase an apartment for each of the four children. The son said that just few days before, a $25,000 check from his father, as a little gift, had bounced. I informed him, that he might consider meeting with legal counsel and his father's primary care physician.

The board application was submitted with the financial statement and documentation of $3,000. Within a day, the managing agent contacted the buyer's broker, asking if perhaps there had been an error. At the same time, the buyers' attorney was informed that something had been terribly wrong.

For the family, they were devastated with the news, when it was confirmed that the stock did not exist and then, worse, that their husband and father was diagnosed with early onset Alzheimer's. Sadly, yet fortuitously for the family, the seller's mother was in the latter stages of the same devastating disease. She was very understanding, crying on the phone that she would immediately instruct her attorney, who advised her against doing so, to return the deposit.

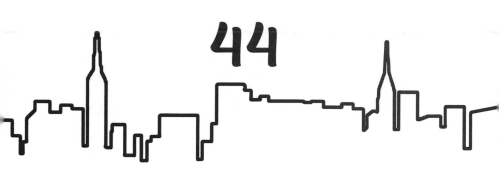

44

Real Estate Emergency

Rosemary was sitting at the kitchen table at the North Main house, scanning and clicking away on her laptop and I was standing by the stove, stirring honey into a cup of tea. It was February 2016, and she still had not gone back to Sicily since returning to New York for the holidays, was still spending weekends at our rental house, all of us still having work to complete on our houses. Alfred was gaining on Paul and me. We had shut final construction down on our house to use it for the summer season. The master bedroom and bathroom, the pool, pool house, and landscaping were all done and perfectly comfortable.

"This is it!" Rosemary had suddenly burst out. "I had this strong feeling." She picked up her cell and was pressing numbers. "A house on Walnut! It's going into foreclosure! Hello? Oh hi, this is Rosemary Renna. I'm a broker, by the way, but this is for myself. I'm interested in the house you have advertised. Mm-hmm . . . I see. So you took highest and best offers this morning? Do you have a signed contract? May I call you right back?"

"Which house?" I asked, joining her at the table.

"Seventy-One Walnut."

"That's the house I went to go see with Paul and Daddy. We were there nearly four years ago. In fact, Daddy actually peed behind the bushes."

"That's a sign. It's going to be my house! He never peed outside. Okay, the broker said they already have three offers at the full asking price, two are all cash."

"With some owners that means nothing if there's no contract. Buyers can and do walk away. What's the ask?"

"Nine hundred forty-five thousand and there's no contract."

"Okay. You told her you're a broker. To her that means a co-broke, so right off you need to tell her that you are not taking a commission nor a referral fee, and you need to make a big enough jump over the asking price to discourage those incremental five-to-ten-thousand dollar increases in a bidding war. Make a solid offer."

"Like what?"

"Nine seventy."

"I'll tell her nine hundred seventy-five." Rosemary pressed redial. "Hi, Susie," she said, as if they were already great friends—it's a really good negotiating tactic. I listened and mouthed a few reminders. She added that she would pay all cash, and did not need to see the property as family members already had and for her it was all about location. Clearly she was getting some resistance and I was sure it was because the other offers did not include another broker. That meant Susie was losing money at this juncture on a house she and her partner tried to sell on and off for years. I repeated to Rosemary in a stage whisper to take her brokerage side off the table. Finally, she did. The door opened a bit wider.

"Oh, I see you're with Elliman," Rosemary said. "My brother is Alfred Renna. Do you know him?" I tried to sit still as Rosemary gave a few more mm-hmms, knowing what the broker was saying— they all know Alfred; they all love Alfred. Things were going better. Susie was going to call the owner's attorney. "So who is the owner's attorney? Can you give me that information?" Rosemary wrote down the name. "So let's talk again in a little while, and I'll call my attorney. Do you know Michael Renna? Yes, he is. Yes, he is a great guy and a great attorney—and still single." Like Alfred, our cousin Michael was handsome and everyone always asked whether they were single. We had given up on fixing either of them up on dates. Rosemary hung up.

"Okay, so she's giving the attorney your offer?" I asked.

"Yes. Now I need to call Michael." She was pressing his number. "Michael!" She had him on speaker. I was barely breathing.

"Rosemary," he answered way too slowly and calmly. "I'm on my way to meet with your brother for lunch."

"This is a real estate emergency!" she spit out, then quickly filled him in on what was transpiring. Nevertheless, Michael—who had been hoping Rosemary would come back to Southampton and buy another house, as she was his favorite cousin—answered in a very measured way.

"This is a real estate emergency. Are you at North Main? I'm just about to drive by." In one minute, he was parked and standing in the kitchen, a rush of winter air coming in behind him. Rosemary and I, no longer able to sit, were pacing. She pressed Alfred's number and put him on speaker as he answered. We could hear power tools in the background.

"Alfred, Cousin Michael is here." She said immediately.

"What is Cousin Michael doing at North Main?" he asked over the din.

"Hello, Alfred."

"Oh, hello, Michael. You're supposed to be meeting me at my house."

"Rosemary has a real estate emergency," I blurted, unable to contain myself any longer. We all filled Alfred in.

"This is a *real* real estate emergency. I'll be right over." In two minutes, Alfred came through the back door with another blast of cold air and stood in the kitchen with the rest of us. We needed some intervention. On the way over, he had already called Susie to reconnect and assure her that Rosemary had the funds to close immediately or whenever was desired. In the meantime, I suggested to Rosemary to send her bank statement to the broker along with her offer, with all terms, in writing. Michael was expressing his concern for having an engineer's report as a contingency. I knew that wouldn't fly and got Paul on speaker to see what he recalled about the basement, the first place he always looks when we view properties.

"It will need all kinds of work sooner or later, but nothing we can't handle."

"Michael, Susie gave me the seller's attorney's name. Maybe you know him." She read the name off her note. Michael didn't but Alfred did.

"Oh! He's a good friend of mine. I'll call him right now. I won't ask him favors—that would be unethical—I'll just let him know you're my sister and that you have the means to close, to make him and his client feel comfortable, since they probably don't know these other buyers." He went off into the other room, and we could hear him chatting and laughing before getting down to business. We were all feeling good. Susie called a few minutes later to suggest Rosemary visit the property.

The house had been illegally divided into several small apartments, each occupied by local workers who may or may not have had their green cards. Everything was spotless and orderly, and everyone we met was lovely. They all were concerned about trying to find other places to live. Eventually, Rosemary told the young family on the second floor—who had just come to our country and who had three young children in the local school—that they could stay through the end of the semester, in spite of the fact it would hinder her ability to fix the house up in time to rent it for the exorbitant summer rental it could bring. They expressed their gratefulness through their beautiful twelve-year-old daughter, who translated from Spanish. She had been speaking English for all of three months and she was brilliant.

After viewing the living quarters, we went down to the dark, dank basement, where there was about seventy square feet of standing room, the rest being barely a crawl space. It looked all of the 150 years plus that it was . . . and then we spotted it: our mother's name written in crude uppercase lettering on one of the ancient beams brushing the tops of our heads. MILLIE. Rosemary was ecstatic that it was yet another sign she would win the contract on the house. Not only did the house that we all thought our parents should have bought years before have our father's DNA in the soil, but it also had our mother's name on a rafter. We were all getting more excited. We were also feeling the growing demand in the market to be a few steps from Main Street, despite the rising numbers of for-sale signs and open-house balloons everywhere else. It seemed there were more spec houses than ever—overly big houses built by hopeful developers, some of whom had the perfect summer house formula and others who didn't.

After numerous hurdles to preclude the auction date at the courthouse, two days after Rosemary submitted her offer, the bank agreed to the owners going into contract with her instead.

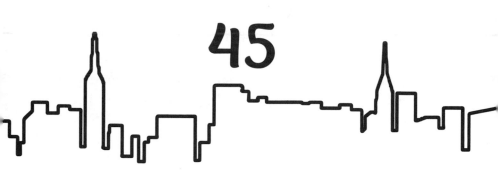

45

Peel-and-Stick Moldings

Alfred had stopped by my apartment on his way to dinner in my neighborhood. He was telling me that he had been helping one of his brokers who was having difficulty selling one of his exclusives. Apparently, the broker wasn't sure how to address one of the house's design features, which was the least of the issues the property had.

"May I use your computer?" Alfred asked, plopping into a chair in my kitchen and sliding my Mac over. "I have to get back to a broker who called earlier to discuss his molding issue—he's having trouble getting anyone to even look at his listing, let alone getting any offers." He was not getting even a single *looky-loo*. We actually don't mind a few of these folks showing up at open houses. We have seen several of the same ones over the years, and they have no intention of buying. Looky-loos just look. Still, they boost the number of bodies that come through the door, and more lookers help a property appear more desirable.

Alfred found the listing under *town houses*. The broker's head-line read "Downtown Town House." The description went on to say that it had been totally renovated three years prior. It sounded like an amazing opportunity for the price, as I was picturing federal fab-ulous, West Village quaint, original moldings, and fireplaces on all four levels, and all lovingly restored with a perfectly planted garden in back. He went to the photos next. The first shot was of the liv-ing room and we noticed, in the background, that the front door had little windows up at the top, more reminiscent of Queens. The decor of the living room was like a boudoir. There were paintings of Victorian women draped across chaise longues in various positions. In the middle of the room was a Victorian-style dining table with ornate, black cast-iron legs and a pink marble top. It sat in front of a carved-wood-framed love seat, painted gold with pink, tufted upholstery. Alfred immediately got the broker on the phone.

"Why does the living room look like a boudoir?" I could hardly imagine the answer. Alfred put his phone on mute and said, "He's asking, 'Is it that bad?'" and rolled his eyes. "He says they love it." He scrolled to the next photo and took his phone off mute. "Is the small, white room with the overstuffed, black leather sofa and dead deer head on the wall the man cave? How did I know?" Alfred muted again. "He's young. What does he know about man caves?" Then he unmuted it again. "Okay, so what about those moldings? I've never seen anything quite like them."

I watched Alfred's face for his reaction.

"Mmm. I'm not sure I've ever heard of peel-and-stick moldings." He turned back to me biting his lip and muting again. "Joanne, have you ever heard of such a product? And they want millions for this." We expanded the photo to take a good look. The moldings had to go. He pressed his phone so he could speak to the broker again. "Listen, the moldings have to go, and so do those little chandeliers. There are chandeliers galore. It's a distraction."

Next we looked at an exterior shot that we were certain was a mistake. It was a redbrick, two-story, older postwar apartment building divided into several two-level apartments. "Jack, you must have the wrong exterior shot. This must be Queens, like maybe Jackson Heights or Elmhurst." The broker assured him it was the correct shot and that there was a whole row of these Downtown. In Queens, they're called *garden apartments* even though no one has a private garden. Most tenants do put lawn chairs outside their doors. In Manhattan, there is no classification for them.

I continued to listen, curious about what he was going to advise. He told Jack that there has been no interest because, first of all, it is not correctly categorized and not showing up on apartment searches. Second, calling it a town house raises the buyers' expectations; it's really more like an attached garden apartment. Third, while the exterior couldn't be altered, the interior needed to be staged and new photos taken. Last, he addressed the price. It had been valued as though it was a town house, asking in the high three-million-dollar range, rather than what it really was: a two-bedroom apartment without a doorman, where you'd have to shovel your own snow. Alfred told Jack that I was sitting there with him looking at the photos and switched to speaker, so Jack could tell us about a prior offer. He spoke in an excited voice.

"Hey, Joanne, thanks for your input. Listen to this. Last year a developer approached the co-op, and you should know that every one of these units is the same space, combo living/dining on first level, small staircase to second floor, two bed, one bath. And he offered each shareholder nearly five million dollars! Crazy! There were nine owners, and seven wanted to take the money and run, but two held out for more. Before he scrapped the offer, the plan to was to tear it all down and build a high-rise."

It was a lottery-winning kind of offer that got canned because of two holdouts. Alfred ended the call saying he'd get back to him with numbers he thought would make sense. We both agreed the value had to be compared to other co-op buildings, making adjustments for the lack of services. Its uniqueness to Manhattan did not add to its value. We concurred that the asking price should be in the $1.65 to $1.7 million range, and even at that, we were skeptical. Alfred's final words to the broker were, "Tell your owner, one decorates to live; then you decorate to sell."

It was a few months before we heard the results of Alfred's conversation. Jack convinced the wife that staging to sell would be to her advantage. She thought she would be the best person to tackle the project. She did have the offending stick-on crown moldings removed, and rather than spackle and paint where the Sheetrock had pulled off, she put up an easy-stick wallpaper trim in an art deco design. The deer head and black leather sofa were moved to the living room, though the pink-marble-topped table remained. New photos were taken, and those of the exterior were removed from the listing. While the price was dropped a few times, it was never at a salable level. When a seller could have gotten $5 million, it is difficult to accept something so much lower. While this had been perhaps a once-in-a-lifetime offer, the sellers believed they could sell it at more than its actual value. They tried another broker hoping for a different result, but last we heard, the property was permanently off the market and the owners were mid-construction on a complete renovation. The wife had been inspired by a recent condo called the Waterford and was duplicating the kitchen of that building . . . and adding more chandeliers.

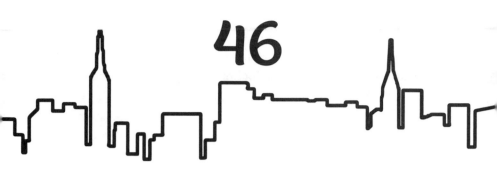

Trends from Chandeliers to Moldings to Polka Dots

For a few short years, moldings fell off the desirable-detail list. I had a lovely, full floor, prewar, twelve-room apartment on Park Avenue that had been an estate and not touched for over thirty years. The elderly couple who purchased the apartment spent nearly two years completely renovating it. The apartment needed things that did not exist when these buildings were built, such as central air-conditioning and sound systems. It also needed all new electrical and plumbing, new plaster walls, then all of the original crown and base moldings, door and window trim, pilasters, fan-shaped transoms, and so on (which were in poor condition), needed to be recreated by artisans. A few short months later, the new owners decided to move to Palm Springs, and I put the perfectly renovated home, with all its deep moldings slicked with oil-based paint, back on the market. The photos and brochures were stunning, yet the first words out of every buyer's and decorator's mouth was, "Ugh, these moldings have got to go." The new quarter-sawn herringbone floors were "too brown; we would have to have them bleached." Another buyer, the heiress to a fashion mogul's empire, took one look and stated, "I'm all about low, white furniture. I would have to have all the floors painted black, and that mantel has got to go." Not one buyer appreciated the prewar design. Finally, one day, a young couple walked in and fell in love. It was their dream home and they would not even need to paint. Best of all, they knew someone who knew someone on the board and passed with flying colors.

With so many cultural influences, buyers and their decorators have again embraced moldings, but with choices. We can go all the way, with crown and base moldings, or we can choose to go base molding only, with a nod to traditional, and that looks good juxtaposed with modern furnishings and art. Base molding with no crown molding mixes it up and gives it a modern architectural touch. We can choose no moldings with walls that appear to float a mere half-inch off the floor, against which a fabulous, carved, antique sideboard would sing, as would a midcentury console, and still be trendy. It costs more to build that way but looks really cool.

Many of our design decisions are influenced by the European look that has come on like a wave, and there are two versions: northern as in Northern Lights, and southern as in warm Mediterranean sun. The Danes and other Scandinavian design divinities have turned their scrubbed floors and original midcentury bent-wood lounge chairs into the hottest look, and with or without moldings, it looks fabulous. The esthetic is spare, such as a one-bulb light fixture perfectly looped over an old beam. There's a trace of Spartan introspection that we New Yorkers find ethereal and sexy; we might even fantasize about the long, dark winter wrapped in roughly woven blankets and sheepskins, getting our fill of sitting before a crackling fire and warming our hands on thick mugs of hot glogg.

Head south to the Mediterranean warmth, and we find two-foot stone walls, huge beams from trees that grew back during the Roman Empire, and ancient parquet juxtaposed with slick, white leather and polished chrome legs. Then, our fantasies turn to what it would feel like to be perhaps the ninth generation to inherit such design splendor and step through doors flung open to dine alfresco on worn marble verandas, where the olive wood dining table and tapestried chairs have been brought outside, because why would we use anything less magnificent?

The most southern reaches of Italy have ancient structures influenced by both Greek and Middle Eastern design. Painted tile floors from centuries ago look new today. The Greek key motif has influenced every decade of divine decor. Virtually every culture can be mixed with another culture for spectacular interior inspiration. Our design taste and approach becomes more cultivated as we are exposed to so many design and real estate television shows and websites that illustrate how to research what has been done and tweak it to look new and feel fresh and exciting. Contrasting furnishings can harmonize when put together in powerful combinations. Done high-end or tag sale, a transcendent Italian light fixture can ignite a room. A glitzy chandelier that once hung over your great-grandmother's dining table might make your powder room sparkle with design brilliance.

Our interior design choices speak volumes about who we are, what we aspire to be, or who we want the world to think we are, and that includes what we put on the walls. Just like moldings, what hangs between the crowns and bases trends up and down. Polka dots had their day, as well as harsh spotlights to illuminate your art, also known as *wall washers*.

Polka dots that look like old-fashioned candy are also known as Damien Hirst *Spots*, as he painted a series of them titled such. They are simply circles of different colors that form a grid. The artist had been known to say that he painted them simply for "the joy of color." Owning a Damien Hirst painting became very cool from 2005 to 2008, especially if you hung one in your home as a delightful contrast to more serious pieces in your collection. They were also a sign of currency—that you had lots of it. Since 2012, the value of Hirst's work has plummeted, but before the art world downgraded their value, brokers and designers had already been whispering that the spots had gone from edgy to quaint. They had been hanging all over, from Park Avenue to Crosby Street. If they're still on your walls, it's time for them to go down to the storage room. But like the stock market, there are the contrarians who bet on market swings. Currently, savvy dealers and collectors are hoarding Hirsts in hopes of a spectacular recovery.

Black-and-white photography in a carefully curated collection, especially from the 1950s and '60s keeps on looking good, especially if they are from European photographers and capture the essence of Europeans in their towns. Even though it's now decades later, we like sitting in cafés, gazing into store windows on wonderful avenues, leaning over bridge railings to look down at rivers, and admiring stylish people smoking (even though we don't like smoking).

Sant Ambroeus in Southampton has a great black-and-white photograph collection. Hidden-away hotel bars have black-and-white photographs especially fabulous juxtaposed with darkened-with-age wood paneling. We love them. But personal photographs are another thing altogether. Seeing all sorts of cute, sterling silver frames sitting on various living room surfaces carefully placed in clusters looks contrived. The elderly couple who bought, renovated, decorated, then sold their beautiful twelve-room spread had their family photos filling the hall to the staff rooms. She had been a movie star and he was a well-known movie producer, so there were some pretty and famous faces. There in the center of the wall was a small photograph of a civil rights march with the husband, who started out as a young journalist, his arms linked with Martin Luther King. I would stare at that photo in awe every time I showed the apartment. I loved it. It was a great historical photo.

But as for the usual clusters, well, for brokers and their buyers, it gives them the chance to scope out who the seller is, but let's face it, no one is impressed with those ski-slope family shots, or the sunset on the Caribbean beach photo used for last year's holiday card to show you went on a very expensive family holiday. The slopes, the shore, and the litany of fundraiser photo ops with presidential hopefuls should be hung on one wall in a back hall.

Oversized, contemporary digital photography that looks like abstract art or scenes that create depth or distance still look good. We love those endless, digitally-enhanced beach scenes that everyone with a duplex hung in their soaring stairwell. But it's time for something new to aspire to acquire. They're all over the place because it was trending.

My family and I have admired graffiti long before it hit the galleries and made street artists into art stars. Great graffiti still looks wonderful, whether on a Brooklyn warehouse wall or on yours. It epitomizes city living, full of energy, color, and the signs of speeding life. Graffiti on upholstered furniture is out! It lasted two minutes. So are art books that cost as much as original artwork sitting on your coffee table. They are dust collectors that will end up on the heap with those old Norman Rockwell books. No one wants them. Let's start right here with saving the planet—no more art books that could double as a Ping-Pong table.

Edgy, pricey, and even ugly lighting that looks like expensive art pieces hanging all over: living rooms, dining rooms, bedrooms, closets, bathrooms? I love them more each day. And must we see one more Saarinen pedestal table reproduced by Knoll in every home, staged or not? Yes! Why? Because no one has designed a better table. We love them. They are the essence of form and function, a perfect design. I've got one in my city kitchen, along with four Tulip chairs. With the standard tabletop, Knoll's version of Formica, and with my friends and family discount, it still cost an arm and a leg. I've been fantasizing about acquiring a big oval one with the top made of Calcutta Gold marble for Southampton.

Abstract paintings? We all love them. Bill Fischer abstracts? We all have one.

We also love abstract impressionism and would love to see a new wave of artists exploring that. Conceptual, video, and performance art is all provoking, and we enjoy the experience of it, but it's hard to live with. Plus, how well does conceptual work really stand up to the test of time? It has to be very immediate to be relevant. Last year I saw a piece in a Fifth Avenue penthouse that was a Plexiglas box hanging on a wall of the grand foyer, and it was filled with Botox vials glued to a canvas. By now they're probably falling off, which may have been a part of the artist's message. The trend to collect conceptual pieces or installations does two things: it makes the collector appear to be cutting-edge, an explorer of waters only the very select can understand, and it implies wealth. To be in the club, you need lots of money and a museum-quality collection that boosts the values of the new hot artists coming to the market.

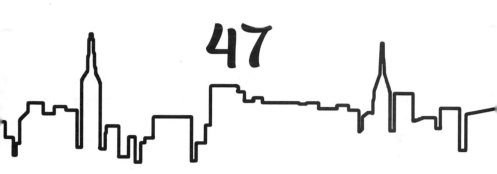

Obsessive-Compulsive
Design Disorder

"Alfred, what are you doing?" I asked. He was at the table in the North Main house kitchen with a pile of little cardboard squares and rectangles that he had cut out from a pie box with dull scissors and was moving them around like a jigsaw puzzle. Our craft supplies at North Main are very rudimentary.

"I'm laying out the bluestone pattern for my patio."

"You've been at it for days."

"I hate all the tiny pieces they're putting down."

I didn't want to say anything, because my stonework is stunning, two-by-three-foot herringbone with glazed edges and perfect quarter-inch mortar. Let's say I wasn't impressed with his mason and his caveman tools over at Herrick, aka Alfred's house. Eventually, the builder had to fire the guy, pull up all the stone, and start all over.

"Very nice. Looks way better with the larger pieces of stone mixed in," I told Alfred. "When do you want to look at tile for the lower level?" These spaces are more than just another spillover illegal guest bedroom. If a basement has Southampton legal egress, it's counted as living space.

"You mean the basements? Don't overspend on a basement. A basement is a basement is a basement. No one wants to go down there. When was the last time you went to the basement of any open house we've been to? Joanne? None, that's how many," Alfred said.

The lower levels of big, new houses in Southampton now include anything from extra bedrooms, yoga rooms, wine storage and tasting rooms, music studios, gift-wrapping rooms, home theaters, and game rooms. The finishes are just about on par with the rest of the house. Those with large enough properties and bank accounts create walkouts. These are enlarged areas excavated to basement level, and made into patios, courtyard, and gardens, accessed from the lower level rooms of the house. An egress is mandatory to consider a basement as legal living space. There are dual-lane lap pools and dual bowling lanes, but for our more modest houses, Alfred and I were each opting for an exterior staircase, inviting laundry room, a spot for an extra-large television screen, a tough-fabric sectional for visiting kids, and one overflow guest bedroom.

We were finally getting our coats on to search out lower-level quality flooring that could go on top of my radiant-heated floors. Rosemary stayed behind to work on table designs, and Alfred and I hit all the local tile showrooms, including one with such bad lighting that nothing looked good, including us. I also made the decision to go with lower-level, quiet, artistic light fixtures. Needing a design fix, we drove over to Sag Harbor, the haven of fabulous midcentury furniture and the latest in lighting fixtures boutiques. We spent the rest of the afternoon meandering through *Architectural Digest*–worthy rooms, breathing in the scent of fine Italian leather couches—which are always on trend—and sitting in very expensive, very soft sheep-skin, upholstered lounge chairs that no one will want another year from now.

The next day, Gina was planning to drive out to Southampton to check on her two houses, hang a permit pending sign on Harvest to construct a garage, should any potential buyers request one, and come by North Main for drinks and a snack, but we asked her if we could go over to Harvest earlier, to steal ideas from her—we all love her design eye. Alfred already knew where the key was hidden, having gone over a few times to try and get a handle on what stain his floors should be. We had both been carrying around big squares of floor samples in our trunks for months; our floor man is long-suffering. We had visited him a dozen times, and that was just for Alfred's house. Surprisingly, I knew exactly what I wanted for mine and had not changed my mind once—wide board oak, slightly brushed with a whitened wax finish that reminds me of a perfect cappuccino.

It started raining when we got to Gina's house, so Alfred and I donned the blue shoe booties that surgeons use that she had by the door, and took a photo of our feet to text to her, so she knew we were being careful not to track water and mud all over the house. After an hour, we were still discussing what we would do differently and that just maybe the house actually had too many windows. As we do with all houses we look at, we could not help but redesign it in our heads. It's a compulsion. I'm sure Gina does the same. Nevertheless, there were virtually no open houses that weekend, so this would help our hankerings. Of course we also spent hours looking at Alfred's project, my project, and many hours searching online for light fixtures, sofas, and cocktail tables. Our only break from designing was baking cookies and bingeing on our mutually chosen TV series that none of us had yet to watch.

Back at North Main, we could hear Gina coming in through the back screen door. Most everyone uses the back doors in Southampton, probably because it's more a summer place and everyone is out back by the pool. If no one is home, grab a bottle of chilled water, take a dip, or head over to the beach if you have a parking permit, because that's where everyone is.

"Hello." She clunked in with fur-trimmed and -lined Gucci clogs. "I thought these shoes would keep my feet warm on building projects. Alfred, my feet have been frozen since we were at your house last week. I hope no one is offended by my mink fur coat." No, we weren't, even though it was so voluminous it took up half the living room.

"Put that thing in the bedroom."

"Oh yeah, I think I remember where it is . . . Found it!" I like to think she was inspired by our bedding of many patterns, which came from a great import store in the village; she had done nearly the same combination in one of the bedrooms in her spec, only I had found the comforter she used at Target.

"I saw everyone's cars," she said, coming back in the room "Oh— you have company." Michael came in the back door just as we were grabbing a tray of vegetable sushi, a bowl of cashews, and some chilled Prosecco. Perfect timing. We were excited to introduce him to Gina.

"Cousin Michael, meet Gina. We've decided to adopt her as another Renna."

"Hello, Gina."

"Hello, Cousin Michael!" Introductions done, we planted ourselves in our big, white sofa and chairs in the living room for an intense session of real estate conquests, negotiating victories, and each of our obsessive-compulsive design disorders.

"You see these side tables, Gina?"

"Yeah . . . you got them at the English place?"

"They were one thousand, three hundred, and fifty dollars each over there."

"We loved them because they added architectural interest," I added.

Alfred continued. "The first time we saw your spec on Burnett, I took a photo of a tag hanging on your dining table. It was company called Noir. We called, said we were designers, used Joanne's resale number, and got these for a fraction."

"I know. You also bought those chairs in the kitchen from me. They're from Noir. I use them a lot. But I shoulda kept this coffee table. What did you pay me?"

"Four hundred bucks."

"That was a steal. What about those lamps—hey, I like your Christmas tree. It's minimal."

"We only hung one layer of ornaments. The rest of the decorations are ribbons from Christmas presents and cookies from Sant Ambroeus."

"So, Gina, I'm redesigning my stone patio," Alfred began.

"Can I tell a real estate design story?" Michael interjected. "I mean since this is like group therapy or Design-aholics Anonymous?"

Everyone agreed and gave Michael the floor. "Well, Alfred and I bought a three-bedroom condo corner unit here in the village, and decided to renovate and stage it before selling. So first we bought a ladder, and I went over there from time to time to do a little painting. Then Alfred and I bought two beach chairs."

"And we'd go and sit for a while." Alfred added.

"Yes," Michael continued in his measured way, "and if it was warm enough, we'd take our chairs out to the patio and have a couple of beers. I had put a case in the refrigerator for our visits. So, one sunny afternoon as we sat outside, and by the time I had one wall painted, we heard from the broker." He stopped to allow Alfred to continue.

"So we get a call from the broker who sold the unit to us, and she had a buyer who wanted a corner unit."

"But Alfred told her we really didn't want to sell. Go ahead Alfred, tell everyone what happened next."

"The broker called again and asked what it would take to sell. I put her on mute to discuss and we agreed, it wouldn't take anything, we didn't want to sell. I tell her so but then she asks what if she got us one hundred thousand more than what we had just paid for it. We said no."

"Every time the broker called, the number went up." Michael added with a chuckle.

"When she got to one million dollars, we finally looked at each other and said, Are we crazy? We could go have beers at Fellingham's."

"So we took a vote, two to zero, to accept the offer."

"And we sold it at a three-hundred-thousand-dollar profit, after only three months from the time we bought it."

As we sat and talked, I realized it felt like one of those weekends that spin you around, and as fun as that might be, you're not quite prepared for Monday. As if it would be more relaxing, getting away from all of our Southampton projects, I suggested to Paul that we should head back to the city early and have the family over to our apartment for meat sauce over pasta. Everyone agreed to come.

Back in Manhattan, later that evening, we had a great family meal and attempted to discuss everything except real estate and design, in an attempt to clear our minds. When it was time to clear the plates, Rosemary was examining my living room. She just couldn't help herself.

"Joanne, let me help you and Paul redecorate this apartment. You have the most fabulous space, you've got these high ceilings, and you haven't done a thing in years."

I looked around and it was true—I hadn't done anything except replenish the many candles we used for sit-down dinners. "We need to complete the Southampton house first. We're almost done."

"You can't wait any longer. Look at that piece over there. What is it?"

"It came from a client whose apartment we sold. I think it's a buffet."

"Joanne, Rosemary is right," Alfred said. "What is that? Mao Tse-tung meets Ralph Lauren?"

"The sofa is Ralph Lauren. It's a great sofa," I said, defending it.

"Alfred, she's right. That is a great sofa, and it looks good right where I moved it after Jonathan died."

In a few moments, Rosemary had pushed the black, red, and gold buffet piece with strangely flaring legs, my nod to 9, out into the public hallway, where it looked oddly right at home. The corner of my living room suddenly had new life. "Alfred, hold up the end of the cocktail table. I'll yank this carpet out."

"I like that carpet, Rose."

"It doesn't work." And out it came from my conversation corral as I've heard one of our friends and decorator call that space where an area rug creates a room within a room and seating is pulled in close. "This place needs to look more like a loft." They pulled it out to the foyer.

"Do we like it?" Donna asked with an expression just like our father when he did not approve of something.

"I don't like it," Michael, the practical architect, added. "You have to walk over it from the kitchen to the living room, and to the bedrooms, it's a trip hazard." Quite frankly, I didn't like it much either, the thick, hand-woven pale bluish Chinese rug no longer looked great and was too delicate a color for such a high traffic area of the apartment.

"It will become a mess in this spot."

"You can have it cleaned once in a while." They rolled it up.

Next, they dragged it down the hall and unrolled it in the master bedroom and claimed it did not work. Then they pulled it into the second bedroom that over the years has been a den/sitting room, convertible guest room, painting studio, and the room where everything goes that does not go anywhere else. A few weeks later the room would be filled with tools and stored furnishings, as the Rennas moving a few pieces of furniture and a rug turned into a renovation of scraping, peeling, painting, rearranging, thinning out, auctioning off, and of course finding new occasional chairs, side tables, a white Flokati area rug, and fabulous lighting. Our design and decorating genes had kicked in even though it was late and we were all tired. We were ready to push, lift, hang, shift, and toss, and give the apartment a bit of a less cluttered look, and get it ready for the painters.

Next, they moved into the kitchen and were ready to pull down the wallpaper. I stopped them not only because it was nearly 11:00 PM, but also because it had been hanging for so long that it had gone through a period of being out of style and was just now looking good again, so I tried to convince myself. I even found a website about a designing couple that save your well-worn, real-life look to mix with new cutting-edge or grandmother ethnic stuff. It's a downtown, Brooklyn mix that's organically cool. The wallpaper did come down, along with a century of plaster.

With dinner over, dishes cleared, and a satisfied sense of new design changes to come, the siblings bundled up and headed to their own apartments.

It was time for Paul and me to spend a night alone, to wind down, put our feet up, and binge on yet another series we had no idea existed. Neither of us had watched TV in years, until Loretta had informed us, "It's the golden era for TV!" She was right. Plus, sometimes you just need to be entertained without moving, planning, searching, or changing something, and it just so happened that, for aesthetic reasons, we had recently replaced the fat, old flat screen with a slimmer, wider model.

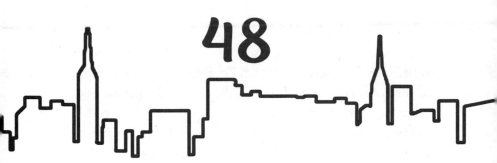

48

Lifestyles and How to
Display Wealth

Throughout history, having multiple children had different con-
notations about wealth. Back in the early 1700s when the United
States was expanding from the original thirteen colonies, having
many children ensured enough hands for the hard work of creating
and maintaining a new homestead. Work included everything from
tending the livestock to farming.[1] And in ancient Greece, women
had many children (male and female) to contribute to the expansion and prosperity of the nation.[2] As of 2016, the average number
of births per woman in the United States was 1.87,[3] but the trend
in Manhattan has been to have multiple children as an indication
of great prosperity, which is quite the investment simply with the
cost to send each child to private school as would be the practice
with the Manhattan wealthy. It is not uncommon to see three to four

offspring in such households, along with a nanny for each kid, and of course, a driver for the family SUV to shuttle everyone about town— work for dad, spin class and lunch for mom, specialty grocery stores for the cook, escorting the kids to school for the nannies as well as playdates, swimming lessons, tennis lessons, ballet lessons, fencing classes, and any other form of life-advancing lessons and classes that cannot be taken in the already-pricey private schools or at home, for the kiddies. Also trendy is having two SUVs and two drivers, so no one should be left stranded.

Another trend for the rich with kids and nannies are the family vacations in very high-end resorts that cater to such groups. Fully staffed vacation houses are built to accommodate parents, children, nannies, and maybe the grandparents. Multiple families arrange for multiple homes to go together during the same private schools' breaks. Depending on whether it is the December holidays or spring break, places like Park Avenue empty out, as all residents head out on leased jets to such places as Saint Barts, Sun Valley, and Cabo. The super-rich are positioned to purchase homes in these areas when they come up for sale.

Wealth display is trending in the form of closets the size of bedrooms, which are the perfect venue for display cases that hold all kinds of collections. I've seen in several tony homes beaded and bejeweled evening bags, such as Judith Leiber, arranged in glass cases like a King Tut exhibit at the Metropolitan Museum of Art. The same with Christian Louboutin shoes, all arranged for the lady of the house to admire as though a priceless art collection. Hermés purse collectors not only display their $80,000 crocodile Birkin bags like trophy heads, but they also like displaying all of their orange Hermés boxes stacked up by size. The apartment stagers covet those boxes to stage walk-in closets. We have a listing now that is beautifully staged, right down to those orange boxes and some white ones with the double *CC*. A competing stager/designer had come to our first open house for a certain property. He works bicoastal and told us about a woman spec-house builder who decided to build a spec house with the idea that a Saudi princess would buy it. So everything she did was in service to this imaginary princess and how much she would love a brushed-sterling silver railing, for instance. Imagine the closets for a princess—they are the sizes of ranch houses. This one had a twelve-thousand-square-foot closet that the builder decided to stage with her own extensive collection of Hermés bags. She then had to hire a security guard to cover the closet door till the house sold. It took four days—and sold to a Saudi princess. It closed all cash the following week. That's what we call specific marketing.

The opposite of overt displays of wealth, or anti-wealth display, is also gaining traction. It is a throwback to those whose wealth was considered "old money" and New England frugal, when the rich would drive a car for so many years that rusted parts would be falling off. It was a time when leather patches on jackets and sweaters started to be fashionable because they added years or even decades of use to the piece of clothing.

Today, it's trendy to throw on whatever is heaped on your floor and artfully wrinkled. It started out West, with the Silicon Valley group, and has been translated into its own Sag Harbor style. We love that puffy down jacket and flip-flops look. It's been warm enough this winter to pull it off. But the spread-your-toes yoga style of sandals on the women just don't make it, unless you're stunningly gorgeous and no one cares because they're looking at your long, bare legs, topped off with a cable-knit sweater. Of course, having an Apple watch is sort of cool, but so are cheap plastic watches. Worn leather straps on a hand-me-down Patek Philippe are even cooler. Sloppy buns for men and falling ponytails for women are in, and some pull them off, but most don't.

The I-just-threw-it-together look has crossed over to interiors. It's not for everyone, but if you have a fabulous eye to pull it off, those in the know will know how cool you really are. We are even starting to see bookshelves again, but now the books and life artifacts have that same wrinkled-on-the-shelves sort of look.

The crossover Sun Valley–billionaire-mogul-summer-camp-casual look is perfect for a cool Hamptons summer day: white jeans, chambray button-down shirt, Chloe flats for women, and if you have one, the official Sun Valley fleece vest, in case it's chilly. You would have had to been one of the billionaires invited to attend the famous Allen & Company conference to get one of these. The 2016 model was dark navy, the year embroidered along with the Allen logo. This year's color code spun off a trend of its own, and dark navy was everywhere—knits, slacks, dresses, and most especially navy-and-white shirts, both plaid and checked. There were a few black leather jackets with black cashmere tops and black jeans with white T-shirts.

Casual yet clearly very expensive dresses by day and bejeweled looks by night have caught on in parts of the Hamptons, especially when your outfit matches your spouse's and the flowers in your garden, which is, of course, perfect for photo ops. Having you and your home featured in any one of an array of "giveaway" summer magazines has been a hot trend for several seasons. You actually have to pay for the editorial coverage, but the story includes details of whatever it is you may be selling. This trend does not seem to be letting up. Some of the newest members to this dress-up club now have their own thing going—wearing six-inch heels and skin-tight dresses, no matter the time of day or night. It's just not working, especially if you have to hobble to your Honda.

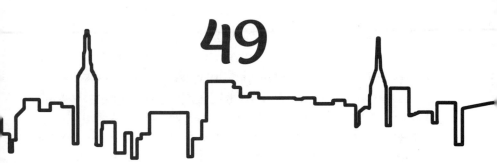

49

Time to Text Good-Bye

B ack in the fall of 2015, I texted Howard Lorber: "Can we talk?" Five minutes later, my cell rang.

"Sorry it took a while to get back to you. I'm in Florida for a couple of days." Throughout the years, Howard has been warm and supportive. At one point, I needed his input on a negotiation for a property where he knew the owner, and he freely gave it. Whenever we saw each other in town or out east, he'd greet me with a kiss and a side hug. Over the years, he'd invited me to Douglas Elliman's tent at the famous horse show called the Hampton Classic. We spent a couple of hours chatting up in his office, but I still needed time.

Just as Rosemary was going into contract on her house that following February, I texted Howard again, and again he called me right away. We made a plan to meet, and that time, I would bring

Donna. The afternoon of our meeting, she and I had decided to get ready at my apartment, then walk to Howard's office, which was two avenues away, rather than have Ed drive us such a short distance. It was a mistake. That evening, we had a windy rainstorm. We both had had our hair blown out, planned on wearing dresses and heels, and had taken way more time with our makeup than usual. We put on sneakers, pulled hoods over our heads, hung on to our umbrellas, and ran all the way. In a corner under his building's overhang, we changed to our pumps, turned our heads upside down to fluff our hair, and in we went.

We spent the next hour and a half laughing. Howard is fun and witty. In between laughter, he managed to tell us why he would love for us to join him. We asked about an older poster of a younger Donald that said TRUMP FOR PRESIDENT he still had displayed in his office. Jonathan and I had seen it when we met with Howard eight and half years before.

About an hour into our meeting, I had taken out a list of requests I wanted to give him. Finally, he said, "Okay, let me see what you've got." At the bottom I had added, "Lunch with Howard." Though I loved working at Corcoran, more and more, I felt disenfranchised. My relationship with its president had become strained since Alfred left. This time, I intended to have a close working relationship with the person at the helm. I watched him nod as he read through each item; then he smiled as he reached the end of the list. "What!?" he boomed in his perfect New York accent. "No dinner?" That's when he had me. I was ready to make the move.

I kept focused on taking one step at a time, and over the next weeks, I needed to oversee the dismantling of fifteen years of files. Each day, Lenny would fill Corcoran shopping bags and take them to the car. He acted like he was a spy. He'd turn the collar of his coat up and put on a brimmed wool hat, pulling the ear flaps down low. As an extra measure, he wrapped a long scarf several times around his head. He was afraid of being caught before we had all of our files out of the office as Corcoran would likely have blocked us and shut us out. They had done just that recently when two brokers decided to leave, also shutting down a third broker who had shared some business with the other two though he had no plans to leave the company. Lenny behaved as though he had contraband and might get arrested! The fact is, we were legally entitled to our files. The worst thing that could have happened is that Corcoran would have pulled the plug.

As we prepared to leave, Ed would be idling just around the corner, waiting for Lenny to put the bags in the trunk. He would laugh and shake his head, getting a kick out of Lenny's disguise. Then Ed would take the bags to my building and leave them with my doorman. My second bedroom slowly filled up. We had computer files to download, we had to wrap the black-and-white photographs of Central Park we used to decorate our office, and we had our own lamps, chairs, computer monitors, and all kinds of desk-top organizers and staplers, tape dispensers, coffee mugs to pack. Lenny slowly removed what was most important to us, moving other things around so the office would not look empty. When he'd come back from dropping the files off with Ed, he'd be white as a ghost and drenched in sweat. He spent most of the time huffing and puffing with nerves, no matter what we said to try and calm him down. In the midst of getting prepared for our departure, we had several listings, all of which were about to go into contract. We didn't want there to be any disruptions to our clients and buyers, but the time was coming when we had to start to inform a few people of our pending move.

One day, David, a colleague and friend, came into the office. He did not notice anything awry. He closed the door and sat down with a serious look on his face. Usually David was smiling and coming in to tell us something funny. We always enjoyed his visits. "I have news," he said with a perfectly straight face. That day he wore yellow cashmere socks with a tweed gray suit, yellow-dotted bowtie, and fantastic handmade English brogues. "I'm leaving."

Donna caught on immediately. "David, are you practicing?" she asked.

"I am," he said with a huge smile. We were biting our tongues not to tell him that we were leaving too. For us, there was too much as stake. Later, too thrilled we would all be at Elliman together, he brushed it off, saying he understood and it didn't matter.

We were the first to go.

Leaving a company after so many years is like getting divorced. You know there are people who are friends who just won't be afterward. Then there are friends who will always be friends. I decided to make our exit as clean as possible. The morning of our departure, April 1, 2016, I prepared a text for Pam, the CEO. It was short. Then I wrote an email for a select few people. These needed to be sent before we would be shut down from our company email, but not before we called the man who had replaced Alfred eight years before. No matter how much he might have liked us, we knew he'd text Pam before we finished our first sentence, and in turn, we knew our systems would be immediately turned off. We were ready. Donna and I got on the phone, then conferenced Bill on his cell at about 8:45 AM.

"Bill, this morning will be our last at Corcoran." We were sad about leaving him behind. I pressed send on the emails, then the good-bye text to Pam, as he expressed his shock and asked if there was anything he could do to keep us. There wasn't. It was time to say good-bye. This time I did not cry.

50

Another One of Alfred's Craziest Deals: You Can't Always Get What You Want

Unfortunately, not everyone gets what they want, and not everyone reacts in a rational way. Certain types of buyers, who see themselves as being high powered, expect all things to go their way. When they don't, a tantrum might ensue. Alfred was helping one of his brokers navigate such a situation.

Sometimes, despite all the hard work of brokers, a deal just goes south. This is about a buyer we'll call Robin Morgan, a Wall Streeter earning $6 million a year. She was the breadwinner in the marriage. Her broker was Amy, and the listing broker on the two-story *maisonette* she wanted was Yvonne. This property faced right into the trees of Central Park, and while it was part of an apartment building, it also had its own door from the street. Robin fell head over seven-inch Louboutin heels in love with it and immediately began negotiations. Let me tell you, she is one tough broad, which she has to be working down in the trenches of the man's world that is Wall Street, as symbolized by the sculpture of a huge bull, not a cow in sight.

Originally listed above $20 million without any takers, the property had been dropped to just under $15 million. There were several interested buyers, but Yvonne negotiated a deal for $13.5 million. Done deal, everyone was on board. Later that same day, another buyer threw in an offer for $13.8 million onto the table. Out of courtesy to the first buyer, the owner agreed to allow Robin the opportunity to match the offer, even though everyone had a verbal agreement.

Robin was in disbelief and didn't trust that the second offer was real, but while considering coming up a little, she became fixated on penalizing her agent and turned the discussion to getting the difference out of Amy's commission. She did not realize how much time she was wasting and what it was going to cost her. By the time she finally agreed to match the 13.8, another offer had come in for 14.25. She was beside herself, yelling, screaming, harassing, threatening to sue, and of course blaming both brokers and most especially blaming Yvonne for having generated a higher offer—though needless to say, it's the listing brokers job to get the highest offer for their seller.

Yvonne, feeling that Robin might still be the better candidate for the building's tough co-op board, suggested that if Robin went up to $14 million, that perhaps she would be in a stronger position to convince the seller to take it. However, the contract had to be signed and delivered by Friday at 3:00 PM.

On Thursday, Robin sent an email directly to the owners of the property suggesting an alteration of the terms to reduce the purchase price by the amount the owners would have to pay on a flip tax, calculated at 3 percent of the sale price, which she would pay, thus reducing the commission and the flip tax because of the lower price. This change caused a delay, and the contract did not reach her till Friday at noon.

With the contract now in hand, Robin thought she was in control and continued to threaten to sue and slander the agents. At 1:00 PM, Yvonne followed up, as was her job for her owner, to be sure the contract was sent back by 3. Wouldn't you know it, Robin just wasn't up to reviewing the contract. After all, she had only just received it—even though she would have had it two days earlier and was single-handedly responsible for all the delays. Feeling empowered, she had her attorney call the seller's attorney to inform them that Robin had gotten food poisoning and would sign the contract on Monday. The seller's attorney, not realizing the backstory, agreed, but unbeknownst to Robin, it was Yvonne who had the seller's confidence, not the attorney. The seller stuck to the deadline.

Now Robin was kicking, swearing, and spitting, and—if she really had food poisoning—vomiting, yet she managed to sign and deliver the contract just thirty minutes past the 3:00 PM Friday deadline which the owners accepted and counter signed. Tuesday evening, as the sellers reread the contract, they noticed the list of occupants. Although the apartment was only in Robin's name, additional occupants included one husband and two cocker spaniels. This was a problem, as the co-op permitted only one pet per apartment. The brokers contacted the managing agent to see if there could be an exception for two dogs; after all, the sellers themselves had a dog, a big one that weighed more than the two smaller ones combined, and the apartment had its own private entrance off the street.

"Two dogs!" the managing agent said. "You're not even allowed one dog. Those owners snuck their dog in!"

Robin was duly informed and has since included the owners and the managing agent on her hit list for those to be sued.

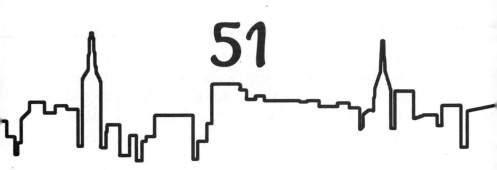

51

Alfred Talks About Pickers, Drive-Bys, and Drop-Offs

We all love searching for great decorating finds. One Saturday, Alfred and I were headed to the other side of the canal, which we must cross over to get from Southampton to Hampton Bays. Alfred was talking about how we had become bargain sleuths and "going to the other side."

The summer of 2016, all four of us found ourselves needing to furnish our latest projects. Rosemary had completed a modest renovation and was madly decorating her new vacation property hoping to have it ready in time for an August rental. It wasn't. I was completely rebuilding my house, adding an additional two thousand square feet and needing all new furniture and lighting and everything else in between.

Donna had just put in a new bluestone patio and was looking for step lighting and wrought-iron tables with chairs for
a landing that was almost complete. Joanne and Paul were
nearing completion on the construction on their house and
had rented a storage room to fill with their finds. We all
overspent on our construction budgets, which had eaten
into our decorating budgets, but being adept at creative
decor, we decided to venture out of the Hampton bubble.
This meant crossing the canal that divides Southampton
from rest of Long Island, essentially making us an island
off an island.

On the *other side*, as we refer to the crossing, we learned
of a whole new world of decorating, what a *picker* was, and
the great thrill of the drop-offs, and James McGuire became
our mentor. We learned of Jim's Hampton Bays shop through
Gina, master builder and stager. Jim refers to his establishment as the "shit shop." It is overflowing with a combination
of goods from estate sales, tag sales, garage sales, yard sales,
and the all-important drop-offs. It's a mishmash of great
stuff, not so great stuff, and stuff we hated last year but love
this year. It is the discarded material of other people's lives
that we see greatness in. We discard too, then find new stuff
to make our surroundings cool, polished, in the finest taste,
but not so far ahead that we look like we're behind. We want
our houses to be *Elle Decor* worthy. We want our friends,
family, and colleagues to *ooh* and *ah* at our fabulousness.

Jim loves to see any one of us Rennas pull up for a fix.
Visiting his shop fills all needs of home-design treasure
hunting, and we love our addiction. At the other end of the
spectrum is his need, the fix to his addiction, to have found
something, negotiated a great price, then turn around and
sell it for a profit.

"The reason I love you guys," Jim said, "is because when you negotiate, I know you are going to buy."

There are so many people who stop by his shop solely for sport. They negotiate, then they don't buy. We're not sure what these folks are called, but the day he said, "You guys are good pickers," we were thrilled. We had shown him a photo of a '70s Plexiglas chandelier that I found on Chairish.com. It had just popped up by a non-dealer, who didn't know what they had, and the price was so low, I didn't even negotiate. I quickly sent the photo to Joanne then called her to tell her how great it could be for her house, but that she had to grab it now; in fact, I just went ahead and purchased it. She had done the same for me a few months earlier when her most favorite lighting show-room in the city was closing its doors. She had found the perfect fixture for my powder room. It had been the clos-est to the one she and I were eyeing over in Sag Harbor, a midcentury French flush mount for $4,000. This one, with her special discount, was $250.

James' eyes lit up at the photo I showed him, and he was already on 1stdibs.com to see the prices of comparable fix-tures. 1stdibs is the most expensive of the sites we peruse, and this midcentury chandelier was featured at over two thousand dollars.

"Joanne," Jim said, "I'll buy it from you if you don't want it. In fact, you guys should be pickers."

He was offering to buy what we found!

"I have a few really good pickers, in fact, you know that lady who was in here a couple of weeks ago, Selma? She's a picker, and she's got lots of money. She picks for sport. By the way, I've gotta show you something I just found today." He started scrolling his inventory photos on his cell.

I had met Selma when I was hunting for a chaise at Jim's to go in my master bedroom. I was upstairs in the mid-century room when I saw a woman I thought I knew. She looked at me as though she thought she knew me. We were kindred spirits. Jim came up and introduced us, and as I asked him about a chaise, Selma stepped right in and said she had several at her home. She gave me her number.

The following weekend, I called her and made an appointment to meet at her home. Joanne came with me. It was worth the visit just to see the perfect light fixture hanging over a round dining table directly in your line of vision as you entered the front door. Neither of us asked who the designer was, not wanting to seem like we were ignorant of such a transcendent item. Selma, who had greeted us in bare feet, white jeans, and perfectly ironed tailored shirt, was anxious to take us directly to her inventory on the lower level for us to see her chaise options. In the dark storage room, where chaises were stacked up, I could not see anything that would work. They were all chrome and black leather, and I was going more for soft, perhaps an upholstered grey linen. I was feeling disappointment when out of the corner of my eye, I saw the perfect piece in her family room.

"Is that for sale?"

Her response was that it could be. I sensed Selma's need, the surging urge that she had to have a fix. She looked at the mushroom-toned Belgian linen and pointed out the mattress stitched cushion. I seized the moment to point out it was missing a button in the tufts. Then she told me that the cushion could be flipped over, which she did in a flash. We could all see a stain on the other side, and she flipped it back over again. I told her that I'd have to have buy all new buttons, and she said I could take one from the stained side.

We pondered. I said that I'd think about it, the signal that we were leaving. She couldn't stand it that she might miss her opportunity for a sale. I had to have the chaise but didn't indicate my building desire. Again, we made a move to head up the stairs and quickly she said okay, and that I could have the chaise for $500. We all knew that it was cheap, really cheap. That Friday, I showed up with cash and a man with a van.

Back at Jim's, he finally found the photo on his cracked phone that he was anxious to show us. He turned the iPhone to present us with the fabulous light fixture he was picking up later that day.

"It's a Hollywood Regency Plexiglas chandelier," he told us. "I already have someone who wants, but I said I had to offer it to you guys first. If you want it, it's yours."

It was perfect for Rosemary's dining room. We quickly called her up and had Jim forward the photo to all of us.

"You would have to tell me today," he said.

We asked if it were possible to see it.

"Okay, can you come back tonight?" he asked. "I'll be closed, but I'll meet you back here. I'll hang it so you can really appreciate what it is. It's a beauty."

We were hooked and agreed to return after dinner and under the cover of dark, looking forward to our negotiation ritual with Jim. How much? This is always our question even when we clearly see his tagged price. What that means is: What is our price? Then we might respond with an eh, that we don't really need it, and do the walk away, giving the impression we're bored with that moment's inventory. When he senses we might really be leaving, he calls out his new lower price, that's when we use the power of how many things all four of us have previously purchased. We hit him with a number, waiting for his response, "That's what I paid, if not more." That's when we know, we've hit his bottom line and where he can still make some money. He's happy, and we're happy. We hate to walk out empty-handed. There are days we've returned twice in hope of a newly delivered lot of merchandise, which Jim is great at acquiring. In fact, for the benefit of his customers who drive by slowly for a look without having to get out of the car, he changes the inventory he keeps out front, letting us all know there's new stuff.

Then there are the promising drop-offs. This is when people pull up with packed back seats and trunks, hoping he will buy off them. We love drop-offs, especially when he pulls a wad of cash out of his deep pockets. Sometimes we might linger for the chance of a bingo quality drop-off when we haven't found anything enticing. There is always at least one other person milling about doing the same.

One day a spectacular, brilliant red floor lamp came out of a van. Before asking the price, Rosemary grabbed Jim's arm to whisper to him that she'd take it. The feeling of a find from a drop-off is like waiting for the lottery numbers to be drawn, and your number comes up. Nothing like buying from a fresh delivery, not yet placed, and before Jim has a chance to check its potential value on 1stdibs.com. He's willing to take the chance on one of our lowball offers, just to keep it moving. The atmosphere of his place is like an open-air Middle Eastern market. A very large, strong man who works for him is always present awaiting the request to move things to better see a hidden item, or on standby for a quick delivery. Jim moves his inventory so swiftly that it keeps us coming back for more.

Needless to say, the night Jim reopened the shop after dinner, for us, we felt like we had VIP status. I suspect you have to earn the privilege. We raced over at the appointed time. It was dark. The shop was dark, but Jim was there, lingering in the shadows. No sooner did we all slip in the door when another bargain sleuth spotted us on his own drive-by and barely missed getting his foot in the door. Jim allowed him in though, another frequent customer and sometimes picker.

Unlike the department stores that open after hours for very famous people, like the Queen of England, to shop unencumbered by mere mortals, there was no champagne for this private shopping expedition, and there would be no negotiating on this subtle glistening find. We didn't even need to ask how much.

"The other buyer wants it bad, but for you guys $750," Jim said.

We said we'll take it, not yet knowing which one of us was even going to use it. It had to be acquired.

Then the following week, what seemed like a miracle occurred. Joanne had still been lamenting over four original Knoll Cesca dining chairs that she thought she had sold at our double-tag sale nearly two years back. The prices for originals had been climbing. While we were lingering for something new to show up, shooting the breeze with our mentor, Paul showed up with a borrowed pickup truck and an old serving piece of furniture from a long-gone dining room set that had been passed from our father's mother to our mother's mother, to Joanne, and then to our parents. We had no idea of its origin or value.

"It's called depression furniture," said Jim, "and was made in the thirties. I don't have room for it. Plus no one wants this stuff."

We were all leaning on the edges of the truck's bed looking at the piece like it was a carcass that washed up on the beach when Paul pulled out his iPhone, that also had a crack, to show Joanne a photo of her four Cesca chairs and told her he must have had his crew put them in storage after the tag sale. She was like a kid at Christmas.

Jim took one look at the photo and exclaimed, "Wow! I'll take them if you can't use them."

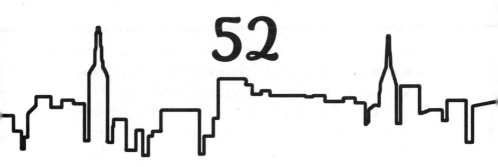

52

Just Another One of Alfred's Craziest Deals: From Boca to Lawn Guyland

Before Alfred left sales to become a manager, he would develop great relationships with his buyers. One of his favorite stories to tell is about his buyer Cynthia.

When I was a broker, Cynthia contacted me to purchase a very special one-bedroom apartment. It couldn't be too prewar, and it couldn't be too postwar. Cynthia was a very successful ad executive for a top ad agency. She was there for twenty years and worked her way up from an ad sales position. Cynthia worked hard and long hours, saving her money, only spending on her wardrobe and jewelry. Twenty years passed and Cynthia, in her forties, found herself alone with a very big nest egg and half her studio turned into a closet. It was time for her to buy. I showed Cynthia apartments for two years! Every time we found the right one, she called her mother, Sylvia, and each time, Sylvia would fly up from Boca to view the apartment and express her opinion.

One time, Sylvia arrived at an apartment Cynthia had not even made a bid on yet, carrying two shopping bags of house-cleaning supplies and a mop. In complete contrast to what was in her hands, she was dressed to the nines, had coifed hair, and was wearing pounds of gold and diamond jewelry.

I asked if I might help carry her bags. Can you just imagine, I was taking them into the esteemed Rockefeller apartments, and she's got two Duane Reade plastic bags filled with rubber gloves, Mister Clean, Soft Scrub, Lysol, and a mop?

"Why," I asked her "are you carrying two shopping bags filled with cleaning supplies while dressed and ornamented like Mrs. Rockefeller on a hot summer day and wearing high heels?"

"I have to break in my daughter's new housekeeper," she replied. I knew she was not planning to do any housework herself.

Sylvia would nix that apartment too before returning to Boca.

Then one day, Cynthia, without including me or consulting her mother, walked into an open house and bought the apartment on the spot, one with a prestigious Fifth Avenue address (even though it's really on the side street and only has a long entry from Fifth). That building is also known for its very inexpensive garage, which includes a free weekly car wash. A favorite building not only for midlife singles but also for divorcees from the Long Island suburban town of Roslyn who want to keep their cars there.

Cynthia, still feeling loyal even though she bought without me, referred her mother's friend, Mrs. Estelle Goldstein, a widow from the affluent north shore community of Old Brookville on Long Island, which she pronounced "Lawn Guyland." Her husband made his fortune in the schmate business, aka knock-off dresses, though Estelle only wore the real designer stuff. Unlike Cynthia, Estelle knew exactly what she wanted, and she wanted out of that bedroom community as fast as possible.

When it comes to divorcees and widows from NYC suburbs, like Estelle, they often think the grass is greener in Florida, but after a few seasons, they'll reach the point that they believe they'll have a better chance finding a husband in NYC because Florida isn't cutting it with all the retirees ogling their young nursemaids, even the retirees who have wives. They will contact several brokers and get on the plane from Fort Lauderdale or whatever Floridian city they hoped didn't have such old, single rich men. In cases like this, the broker becomes both broker and confidant on their new adventure, a willing accomplice to share the sordid details of their divorce, their latest shopping spree, dirt on their former mate's new girlfriend, what a schnook he was, and how bad in bed.

Very much a take-charge lady, Estelle ended up purchasing a large five-room apartment with a terrace on Fifth Avenue. In preparation for her new life in New York and her upcoming cooperative board interview, she also had a facelift. The only call she permitted through to her private room in the hospital was me, her real estate broker. No one else was allowed to call or visit. When I went to visit, I said to her, "Estelle, what a transformation. I will now call you Eve." She loved it.

The apartment Mrs. Goldstein bought was the first I showed her, I encouraged her to make an offer while still viewing other properties, which she did, but she lost it to a higher bidder. Every other property I showed her, she compared to that apartment.

When a buyer loses, you can show them till you're both dizzy, especially set-back terraced apartments, which are a rare specialty property. Luckily for Estelle, there was a board turndown.

Estelle said to me, "Alfred, whatever I have to pay to get that apartment, just tell me. I don't want to lose it a second time."

And so that's when she went to have her face done. I bumped into her at an art opening two years later. I have to say, Estelle was still looking good.

Cynthia's mom, Silvia, was luckier, and found and secured her second husband that winter down south. They decided to purchase a *pied-à-terre* and flew up from Boca to look for a little something. They had a relatively low budget, and I showed them mostly straight-line studios on Second and Third Avenue. Most of them needed work, but Sylvia's idea of work was to have Cynthia's housekeeper come in to clean. The last unit I showed them was well priced for the market and already renovated. The drawbacks were that the kitchen and bathroom were small. She loved the apartment the moment we walked in. She made her way into the separate kitchen. Hubby and I were chatting about the how tight the coach seats were getting on airplanes and how there was never enough room for Sylvia's purse and shopping bags when we heard her call out to her husband.

"Harry, can I toss a salad? I don't know if I could toss a salad in here." Can you just imagine this bejeweled, tanned woman was going to toss her own salad? I went in to see if her elbows were touching the walls.

"Sylvia," I said, "who are you kidding? When are you ever going to toss a salad?"

Right on the spot she decided to make a lowball offer on the apartment and asked me to call the listing broker right away. She could have paid for the whole apartment with a couple of the many diamond encrusted tennis bracelets snug around her wrist. I was thinking, *what does she need those for, she's never been on a tennis court*. The broker answered right away, and I gave the all-cash offer. He mumbled about how low it was. I told him we were still in the apartment and clearly she meant to stay until we had a deal.

"Okay, he's calling the owner," I said.

We were waiting for about twenty minutes, and it was getting warm. Sylvia couldn't stand being on her heels any longer, and I suggested that we wait in the lobby. But no, she wanted to be sure no else could get the key from the doorman, and she was intent on staying firmly in place.

The broker called back with a counter. By now, Sylvia had gone into the bathroom to use the toilet as a chair, as the apartment was vacant. She preferred empty apartments and had actually asked that we only see those, hating to see other people's stuff. She summoned Harry to join her and to close the bathroom door for privacy. I could hear her whispering, then I heard a bit of shuffling, the sounds of bathroom use followed by a flush. She emerged from the bathroom, leaving Harry behind, to give me her highest and best offer. She had come up $2,000.

I was almost embarrassed to call the broker back, but did. We waited for the call back, and she went back into the bathroom to sit again. This time she left the door open, and I could see Harry was sitting on the edge of the tub, sweating, and pressing a wet handkerchief on his forehead. I started feeling bad that I had not turned on the air conditioner. Another twenty minutes went by, and we consumed all of Sylvia's Tic Tacs that she had been dispensing one at a time.

The seller's broker called again to say that if she came up $5,000 more, she could have it.

Her response when I repeated the counter offer to her, "It wasn't meant to be, Harry. Let's go back to Boca."

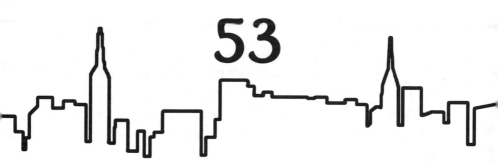

53

A Couple of Breaks

Douglas Elliman expanded, adding another floor that had just been completely renovated. Our team's new office is wonderful. It has southern exposure, and west, across Madison Avenue, we see one of the twentieth century's most important buildings. It was originally called the AT&T Building, then it became the Sony Tower, and is now known as 550 Madison Avenue. It was designed by architects Philip Johnson and John Burgee and has a soaring seven-story portico, suggestive of great Italian arcades, with a set of semicircular arches and a massive, round window placed above the grand entry door. If we press closer to the glass, we can just see the southern edge of Trump Tower, now referred to as "Whitehouse North," and the presidential protection activity on the closed street below. From my apartment's kitchen windows, just west of our office, I have a clear view of Trump's triplex penthouse. I've suggested to Paul, when he might be headed to the kitchen sans clothing, that there are sharp shooters positioned on various buildings, watching the buildings with a clear view to Trump's windows, like ours do.

No doubt life in Midtown Manhattan has gotten more hectic and crowded with the many extra police, Secret Service agents who walk around with "Secret Service" embroidered on their uniforms, bomb-sniffing dogs, heavily armed guards, hordes of tourists and protestors, and true to New Yorker fashion, we negotiate our city, deftly dodging all obstacles and getting to work fashionably dressed and on time.

Our team's new office, right at the center of the bustling activity of selling real estate, is positioned with a straight shot down the broad passageway to the reception area, and a big, soundproof glass door that glides silently closed. Most of the brokers complained though; the desks were smaller, the lights were brighter, and the seats were harder. Okay, I had to agree about the lights. But everyone is settled in now and back to the task of selling apartments.

Again, life offered us new beginnings, and becoming The Douglas Team at Douglas Elliman has a nice ring. Cousin Michael, after many years of saying he'll never get involved again, seems to have fallen in love, and he's already brought the most perfect woman in the world to a family dinner. We all love her. We also had a few curve balls and one ending. The first week of August, Donna had a fender bender; broke up with Michael, who, till the end, showed his humorous side and signed off his last email as *XAmore*; and then broke two bones in her foot following a wild pool party. Without missing a step, she gave all of the stuff her ex-amore had filled her house with to the thrilled landscaper and his crew, sold a bunch of apartments, had a photographers' agent take her on to market her stunning photography, and all of those single men who were holding their breath hoping for a chance were back on her doorstep, negotiating for her attentions. And finally, no one misses Michael's barbecuing at Donna's bungalow—which we decided we love calling her house, as it sounds very '50s Hollywood—because I took over, and true to Renna fashion, everyone claimed it was way better.

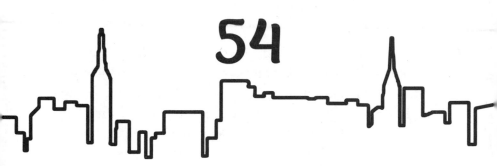

54

The Penthouse Lover

It's unfortunate when relationships just don't live up to one's expectations, whether work or intimate. In regards to real estate, it could be a buyer who drops us after a long relationship. Next we hear, they are off viewing apartments with another broker, still trying to find that elusive perfect penthouse and believing that there was something better just around the corner. Then, there are those buyers who take the step of committing and make an offer, but never sign the contract. They just can't pull the trigger.

Fortunately, with Google searches, buyers like this next one come along very rarely, but even with our internet tools, he slipped through the cracks, not once, but twice! This buyer posed as an independently wealthy investor looking for a fabulous penthouse. His M.O. was to act like he was falling in love with the broker who was showing him apartments. He must have done his homework to be sure he was working with single women. His professing his love easily led to his staying at the broker's apartment "just until finding the perfect penthouse," that he would soon amend should be "large enough for the both of us." This occurred with an attractive, long-single friend of mine until she discovered she was missing money from her wallet and finally tried to find him on Google.

One day, she had come back to the office flushed. It was the first time she took her con man out to view apartments. He had behaved like he had fallen in love with her at first sight. Mind you, this guy was extremely overweight, unkempt with greasy hair, and sloppily dressed. I know because she invited him up to the office on their second "date" out to view apartments, when she needed him to fill out a financial statement in order to make an offer. She was convinced of his wealth and justified his appearance as "eccentric." He went through the steps of negotiating on a penthouse while at the same time he was negotiating his way into her bedroom. She had become so convinced of her love for this man that by the fifth day of their relationship, she jubilantly danced into the office singing, "I think we'll be getting married!" You could see visions of what she thought was his rich lifestyle floating in her head: yachts, jets, penthouse living, and perhaps not having to work so hard. The deal on the penthouse he was bidding on dragged on, and by day seven, he was staying in Julie's apartment full-time. While it was tight for two people, she claimed it a "romantic love nest" and knew that soon they would "fly to their new nest high up in the sky," effusively referring to the apartment he was buying. He used an attorney referred by Julie, when finally there was an accepted offer. The contract process dragged on for three weeks, as he raised all sorts of obstacles. Finally, at Julie's insistence, because he was about to lose the apartment to another buyer, he signed the contract and sent it back to the attorney. Since the 10 percent deposit was then due, he told the attorney that his banker would be wiring the deposit money into the attorney's escrow account. A few days later, the money had yet to arrive. Julie had lost the aura of riches and the glow of love. She had noticed money missing from her wallet and confronted her lover, who blamed the housekeeper. What he failed to realize was that Julie, being very frugal, did not have a housekeeper, which she duly informed him. He became indignant, left the apartment, and disappeared until a year later, when Julie and I were at a broker's cocktail open house for a new listing.

We were milling about, and I had gone to the dining room for some cheese and crackers. While indulging myself, I overheard what an attractive broker on the other side of the table was saying. She was telling someone about her new, rich boyfriend, who had started out as customer and was now bidding on a penthouse for the both of them to live in. She said she couldn't believe she loved this man, who was so out of shape.

I could not believe what I was hearing and had to interrupt.

"Excuse me, Nancy, but I overheard you talking about your new boyfriend." I pulled her aside and asked if she had noticed cash missing from her wallet recently and if the deal on the penthouse was dragging on. Her eyes widened. I suggested she speak with Julie, who had just come into the room. The two of them went into a corner to compare notes, and sure enough, it was the same man. Nancy thanked us both and ran out of the apartment. After she recovered her dignity, she called to let us know that she had informed her doorman not to allow him into the building. She'd dumped the imposter, telling him if he was ever seen again in this town, she'd inform the police.

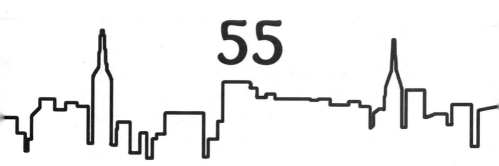

55

Mastering the Market: Reinvent!

Donna, Sherry, and I drove down to the Jersey Shore for Douglas Elliman's annual conference called *Reinvent*. I had never been to Atlantic City and was surprised at a few things. First my BMW 750, which feels like a pickup truck on New York City and Long Island roads, glided at 90 mph over the startlingly smooth highways that led to one of America's Favorite Playgrounds. Second, the ghetto of gambling, drinking, and smoking was also an oasis city of gleaming towers surrounded almost entirely by water, the ocean on one side and wetlands on the other. Last, our rooms, which I had expected to be plain and basic, were glamorous suites with sumptuous beds, large sitting areas, dressing rooms with lots of closet space, and lights so dim you could barely match your socks. The bathroom was a bit brighter, but putting on makeup required extra light from my cell phone, which I also used to check for bedbugs. The room was pristine.

When I met Alfred just before our dinner, which would be for a thousand brokers from all over the country, I asked about how brokers reinvent themselves and what about a company reinventing itself.

"To be a hot company, they need to be part of popular culture, as do brokers," he immediately answered. "There are many ingredients. Elliman, for example, is part of one of the most successful reality shows." He went on to remind me of the day he was at his desk, and a reality show was starting to shoot their pilot at Elliman. The director came into his office thinking he looked like a manager and asked if he would act as a manager in the opening scene, as a way of introducing the new brokers. "I played a pretend real estate sales manager on a reality show about selling real estate, even though I'm a real real estate sales manager."

A few days later, the producers learned about an open house cocktail party for a penthouse. Alfred was in attendance and watched the crew barge right in, camera's running, lights glaring. To one of the participants' credit, the man reminded the director, who was giving orders, that they were in a real open house, hosted by a real broker. The brokers featured on the show had originally been actors, and are now very successful real estate brokers. Reality TV built real real estate careers. TV is great advertising for your business, but there are many other ways to grow. If you have a great idea, explore it, invest your time and energy, and you will find that what you need will present itself. You can find a portal to a whole new way of working. You just need to step through.

That first morning at the conventions' general assembly, Tom Ferry was the keynote speaker for the event. Tom is a self-help author, investor, and founder of a real estate coaching company that has grown exponentially since its inception. He opened our eyes to a new concept of social media and the ability to be a star in our own stratosphere of real estate and brand our own style of sales. Later that day, Donna and I were at the top producers' lunch, where Tom went much deeper into the newest tools of connecting with our customers and creating greater spheres of influence. We were getting hooked on his extraordinary energy and ideas. It was great motivational listening, but the next part concerned whether we were prepared to take a big step and engage with a business coach from his company or not. The better the coach, the higher the cost, which covered four one-hour conference calls per month; access to the Ferry libraries of information, webcasts, and scripts; attendance at top broker conferences all over the country, which also meant great networking opportunities; and a direct line to the latest innovations in technology and marketing.

Donna and I signed up, and we have only just begun to reinvent ourselves and The Douglas Team. The first step was asking for what we wanted in a coach. After going through a few candidates, we were connected with Jeff Mays, a top coach, who talks fast and furious, as he overflows with ideas, methods, and the exact tools to create what he calls "funnels of income." There were two very simple ideas that Jeff shared in the first ten seconds of our first meeting: "You don't have to reinvent the wheel. Take what is already successful out there and apply it to your own business, and if you want to be a one-thousand-dollar-an-hour earner, don't do ten-dollar-an-hour work." Jeff makes us feel like star quarterbacks, motivating us to reach our highest goals.

Next, we used our new team photos and head shots for new Facebook pages and all other social media focused on our real estate business. We want our pages to draw interest, and that means keeping things sharply on point: short iPhone videos showing weekly snippets of our crazy, wonderful life in the Big Apple, along with quick, fabulous shots of our great listings, art openings, design finds, and anything remotely related to real estate.

And finally, we are actively creating new streams of income. In fact, we are about to place an ad on one of the hot websites that everyone checks out such as Monster.com or Indeed.com. Here's what we are looking for in new agents for our team.

Looking for creative, entrepreneurial, multilingual,
and highly motivated agents
to join top sales team
Must have NY State real estate sales license
Minimum five years' experience in real estate sales
We will provide leads
You must be willing to work hard,
have fun, and laugh a lot

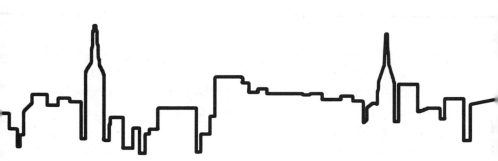

Epilogue:
We Laughed All
the Way Through it

Laughing is truly the most healing action. I wonder: Do dogs laugh? I don't recall our childhood Shetland sheepdog, Dax Van Zandt, laughing. He did want to be in the midst of us when we laughed. Now that I think about it, wagging his tail wildly was how Dax laughed with us. Our father, Alfred Senior, was the straight man. He was always so serious and secretive. We learned shortly before he passed away that he had to be secretive given his aeronautics work and his high-level security status. Our mother, Millie, was beautiful and funny. Along with our love of houses and interior design, she taught us the love of laughter. Our father's straight face and twitching lips only made us laugh the harder, sometimes he'd even bite his lips to keep even a hint of a laugh from escaping. His design sensibility was engineer functionality. When we finally emptied the family home, we found an old light switch over his desk; he had drilled a teensy hole in the black toggle that turned his reading lamp on and off, and added a wire as an extension, so he could switch the light on and off without having to lean over the desk. I can't imagine how tedious it had been and how much time it had taken.

Our parents had kept a big secret until it became too apparent: our mother had been diagnosed with probable Alzheimer's. How did we get through it? We took each stage as she regressed as a part of her life, giving her as much joy as we could. We laughed. We made Mommy laugh. We laughed all the way through it. We still laugh recounting the many stories of all the funny things she did and said.

So we are now four orphans who stick together, even when we can't stand each other and find ourselves bickering. We are all thankful we had our parents for so long. After our mother died, a year later our heartbroken father followed. She was eighty-nine, and he was ninety-two. Till the end, they loved each other unconditionally, always seeing each other as the young, beautiful people they'd fallen in love with. Somewhere toward the end of our mother losing her memory, she forgot she and our father were husband and wife. At one of our many family dinners, she approached us while our father took one of his daily catnaps.

"Have I got news for you!" she said, her eyes shining with excitement. I looked down at her face thinking, *Man, I hope I look as good as she does when I'm in my eighties.*

"What, Mommy?" Rosemary answered.

"I'm getting married!"

"You are?" we all responded like a chorus. It was a mixture of sharing her excitement and a sadness that she was losing who she was.

"Yes! And he's rich!" Our parents' real wealth was their great love for each other, and their children.

We all laughed, and she did too, and that's when we all decided, without even having to say so, that till the end, we would enjoy every moment and Mommy would still be who she was inside. While she lost much, she never lost her desire for beauty and design. When it became too difficult to take her outside, we would help her walk around and around the house for exercise, from the kitchen, through the dining room, and then the living room. We'd have to hold on to her because every time we walked passed the midcentury cocktail table, she had to stop and bend over to rearrange the silk flowers in a beautiful gold-and-white vase. She would mumble and gesture while we hung on, so she wouldn't topple over, and then she would straighten up and look at us with such contentment on her face when the flowers were just right that we knew exactly how happy it made her. So we smiled when she smiled, and she laughed when we laughed, even when she no longer knew who we were or what we were laughing at.

This is who we are. And we all love the same things—great architecture, well-engineered design, wonderful travel and food, and negotiating for real estate. We love to tell stories. We brake for open houses. Most of all, we love New York.

With the Rennas, it is being able to laugh at those stories we love to retell, laughing at our sometimes immature behavior, laughing during the good times, and finding humor even when negotiating the difficult times of life. It is maybe why we always find lots of friends around us. Laughter heals our squabbles; it is difficult to be angry with someone when they are making you laugh. Laughter has also healed our grieving. And finally, after so many years, each of us has our own summer home in Southampton. Most of the time, however, we find ourselves staying at each other's houses for sleepovers.

Acknowledgments

From the both of us: Being on the front lines of New York City real estate gave us the inspiration for writing this book. It all started when Alfred and I were sitting at our favorite outdoor café eating hamburgers, and laughing about a crazy deal on the sale of a ten million dollar apartment. We realized there are so many real estate stories, that we started to write them down. So those people we must thank first are our colleagues—agents and brokers, young and not so young, new to the business or veterans, crazy and not so crazy—we are all connected through the galaxy of selling real estate, from sea to shining sea. We love each and every one of you.

To the team at Beyond Words Publishing, we express our warmest gratitude. You each buoyed us from one step of publishing to the next with patience, grace, and shining brilliance: Nevin Mays,

Lindsay S. Easterbrooks-Brown, Gretchen Stelter, Henry Covey, and Devon Smith. We give our hearts to Richard Cohn, publisher, and Michele Cohn, creative director. Richard, the universe has chosen you to encourage ideas and words that become books! Michele, I get teary eyed at almost every email from you. Not only are you inspiring, you fill me to overflowing with your own expressions of gratitude. Thank you for the idea that the four of us siblings should be on the book cover.

We would not have such life as we have if it weren't for our family. Our sisters, Rosemary Renna and Donna Renna, we thank you for being a big part of this story. Plus, you guys managed to come up with great cover ideas in spite of your bickering. To all of our much-loved cousins and friends who helped shape this book, because you are each a very important part of our lives. If you hang out with us, you know who you are!

From Alfred: To all special brokers and those who have become my close friends, thank you for keeping me grounded and how you enrich my life. A special thank you to two of my dear friends, Daniel D'Ottavio for showing me how to look into the camera, being like a brother to me, and supporting this book, and Anne Chwat, for helping Joanne and me with your legal expertise, guidance, sensibility, and lifetime friendship. And I'd like to thank my big sister, Joanne, for her enthusiasm and drive in the writing of *Negotiating New York*.

From Joanne: My fiancé, partner in life and building, James Paul Joplin, I thank God that he brought us together. Thank you for being by my side, building such a beautiful home for us, and being my computer/internet troubleshooter. Much gratitude to each of my book club friends, and those who read the first drafts, Loretta and Simon Prosser and Isabel and Jonathan Stern, thank you for your enthusiasm, analytic assessments, and great support.

Notes

Chapter 2

1. Leigh Kamping-Carder, "Ranks of Manhattan Brokers Swell, as Market Strengthens," *The Real Deal* last modified December 20, 2013, https://therealdeal.com/2012/12/10/ranks-of-new-york-city-brokers-swell-as-market-strengthens/.

Chapter 48

1. "Becoming American: The British Atlantic Colonies, 1690–1763," Toolbox Library: Primary Resources in U.S. History & Literature, National Humanities Center, September 2009, http://nationalhumanitiescenter.org/pds/becomingamer/growth/text1/text1read.htm.
2. Robert Sallares, *The Ecology of the Ancient Greek World (British History in Perspective* (New York: Cornell University Press, 1991).
3. Central Intelligence Agency, Field Listings: Total Fertility Rates for 2016, https://www.cia.gov/library/publications/the-world-factbook/fields/2127.html.